Heart to Heart—The Journey Inward

Heart to Heart—
The Journey Inward

75 Readings for Lifelong Spiritual Growth

Robert P. Vande Kappelle

WIPF & STOCK · Eugene, Oregon

HEART TO HEART—THE JOURNEY INWARD
75 Readings for Lifelong Spiritual Growth

Wipf & Stock
An Imprint of Wipf and Stock Publishers
199 W. 8th Ave., Suite 3
Eugene, OR 97401

www.wipfandstock.com

PAPERBACK ISBN: 978-1-6667-1667-2
HARDCOVER ISBN: 978-1-6667-1668-9
EBOOK ISBN: 978-1-6667-1669-6

01/06/23

Contents

Preface | vii

Topic 1: Introduction | 1

Topic 2: The Phenomenon of Religion | 9

Topic 3: The Spiritual Journey Part I | 19

Topic 4: The Spiritual Journey Part II | 31

Topic 5: The Five Halves of Life, Part I | 41

Topic 6: The Five Halves of Life, Part II | 47

Topic 7: Death of the False Self and Resurrection of the True Self | 55

Topic 8: Dual and Nondual Consciousness | 64

Topic 9: Levels of Meaning | 73

Topic 10: Perennial Wisdom | 81

Topic 11: The Value of Myth | 90

Topic 12: Personality and Spirituality | 99

Topic 13: Addictive Patterns and Behavior: The Problem | 107

Topic 14: Addictive Patterns and Behavior: The Solution | 119

Topic 15: Spirituality and a Holistic Lifestyle | 129

Bibliography | 141

Index | 145

Preface

In this volume and the next, I examine the meaning and implications of the biblical Great Commandment to love God and others as oneself, considered the core of Jesus' life and message. Here I examine the journey inward, and in the companion volume, the journey outward. Just as there is only one spiritual journey—the journey Godward—so there is only one commandment. Both charges—to love God and others—are fulfilled by love. The human project revolves around love, but it is not human love that is required, but divine love. Because our available understanding of love is almost always conditioned on "I love you if" or "I love you when," most people find it almost impossible—apart from spiritual transformation—to comprehend or receive divine love. In fact, we cannot understand it unless we under-stand it (that is, unless we "stand under" it), like a cup beneath a waterfall. When we come to understand divine love, everything changes, and by that I include politics, economics, and self-understanding.

In the past, we understood divine love as a reward for good behavior, namely, that God would love us if we changed. Such a perspective, however, has things backward. Divine love is not a reward for good behavior, but a call to a larger life, a movement of transformation that results, almost despite ourselves, in different values and behavior. It seems few of us go there willingly. For some reason, we are afraid of what we most want! And the truth is, God does not love us because we are good or because of what we believe, or because we carry the right religious membership. God loves us because God is good.

Divine love is the key to everything. Unloved people misbehave, fail to love, or fail to change. Loved people aren't concerned with rules, regulations, or beliefs. Rather, because they are loved, they take proper care of themselves, and in so doing, become peacemakers, caring for nature and others as extensions of themselves.

Somewhere along the journey of faith, loved people realize that all things are interconnected. According to this perspective, others are extensions of ourselves, and together we are extensions of God. Hence, we love God by loving others, and love ourselves by respecting and serving others.

While the topics of this book and its companion volume—the journey inward and outward—are interconnected, I am addressing them separately. However, as those who live out of the resources of second half of life spirituality know, while society tends to view God, others, and ourselves are distinct, we are ultimately one.

The two volumes of *Heart to Heart*, excerpted from my published writings, consist of one hundred and fifty entries (fifteen in volume 1 and fifteen in volume 2). Grouped together according to thirty topics, each subdivided into groups of fives, entries are designed to be read daily over a seven-month period. While grouped entries can be read in a five-day period over a span of a week, they can also be read in one sitting. If you are willing to commit around ten minutes a day (typically about five minutes of reading and five minutes of pondering or meditation), you will undertake a spiritual journey of epic proportions, guaranteed to transform your faith and revitalize your heart, mind, and soul. In addition, you will come to embrace Christianity as originally intended, no longer as a religion or ecclesiastical phenomenon, but as the transformative movement envisioned by Jesus for humanity, a way of life grounded in compassion, justice, service, humility, and love of others.

Like all great stories, this collection is itself a story, with a beginning, a middle, and an end. Like all storytelling, expect to be entertained, but like all intellectual endeavors, expect also to grow morally and spiritually.

Together with other human beings, each of us is on a journey into the unknown. Whether religiously theists, atheists, agnostics, or simply seekers, each of us is on a journey of faith, spiraling through stages, seasons, or phases of spirituality. As we grow spiritually, our perspective on life, ourselves, and others will change, along with many of our ideas and values. What this means is that even the staunchest life of faith is a life of great change. What may be truth in our youth may turn out to be a lie in our mature years. As poet Christian Wiman notes in his wise memoir *My*

Bright Abyss, "if you believe at fifty what you believe at fifteen, then you have not lived—or have denied the reality of your life."[1]

As those around Jesus discovered (including his disciples and even his mother Mary), the life of faith is one of surprise and perplexity. People who cling to old realities, who compartmentalize their spiritual lives, are left to cling to a faith that is rigid, inflexible, and stale. As Mary discovered, encounters with God lead us out of certainty and into holy bewilderment (see Luke 1:29). Out of familiar spiritual territory, we too are swept into a lifetime of pondering, wondering, questioning, and wrestling. In other words, when our inherited beliefs collide with the messy circumstances of our lives, opportunities arise to progress from idealist, exclusivist, and supremacist forms of faith to realist, inclusivist, and egalitarian forms, that is, from dualist forms of consciousness to unitive consciousness, grounded in humility, compassion, service, and love of others.

Faith is essential to every religious, social, and political perspective, and it stands at the heart of Christianity. The concept is found throughout the New Testament, either as the noun "faith" (*pistis*) or the verb "believe" (*pisteuo*). When we examine the use of these words today, we discover that the common meaning of these words in modern English is very different from their premodern and ancient Christian meanings. When we speak of faith today, we usually have in mind "belief," which we take to mean holding a certain set of "beliefs," that is, "believing" certain doctrines or dogmas to be true. And that modern way of understanding "faith" leads to misreading key biblical texts. For instance, in the gospels, we often get the impression that Jesus insisted that his followers acknowledge his divine status, almost as a condition of discipleship. Those who beg him for healing are required to have faith before he can work a miracle, and one is commended for calling out: "I believe; help my unbelief" (Mark 9:24–25).

We do not find preoccupation with belief in the other major religious traditions, however, so we wonder, why did Jesus place such an emphasis on it? The answer is that he did not. The Greek word translated as "faith" in the New Testament means "trust, loyalty, or commitment." Jesus was not asking people to "believe" in his divinity, but rather was asking for commitment. He wanted disciples who would engage with his mission to abandon their pride, laying aside their self-importance and sense of entitlement, trusting fully in the God who was their father. In this freedom they were to give what they had to the poor, feed the hungry, and spread the good news

---

1. Wiman, *Bright Abyss*, 7.

of God's kingdom everywhere, living compassionate lives. Such *pistis* could move mountains and unleash human potential (Mark 11:22–23).

We begin our evolutionary journey with primal religion, progress through phases of traditional religion, experience moments of skepticism, and conclude with what theologian Dietrich Bonhoeffer called "religionless Christianity." Along the way, we will discover that spirituality is more caught than taught, and that faith, enriched more by subtraction than by addition, is more about unlearning than learning.

In the entries that follow, you will find some negative remarks about the church and its dogma. I am not against organized religion, nor am I opposed to the church per se, but I am opposed to religion as ideology, and to ideology or theology as means of manipulation and control. The church has a positive social role to play, and has accomplished much good in society. Many of us received our moral and spiritual bearings in church, and when institutional religion supplements effective parenting, it becomes a valuable resource. Having attended church most of my life, and having been trained and ordained in the Presbyterian Church, ordination is an office I have served proudly. Organized religion, and the church as a whole, serves many people well, particularly in our formative or first half of life years, but it has largely failed to prepare its members for second half of life spirituality. Like effective parents, the church provides guidance, assistance, and safety for many in society, but its role must also include preparing members for change and ongoing transformation. Effective training means knowing when to let go, and letting go means relinquishing authority, hierarchical domination, and dependence. Above all, letting go means relinquishing control, often maintained through rules, guilt, and threatening doctrines.

In my writings I call myself a "progressive conservative," which means that while I am committed to responsible religious progress and conserving specific beliefs and practices, I am equally committed to change, doubt, ongoing ambiguity, and uncertainty. When I examine my hierarchy of values, my top three descriptors are (1) human (a global citizen), (2) panentheist (a perspective that views God as the container in which everything else is contained), and (3) nondualist (a perspective that opposes either/or thinking because it views all people and things as interrelated extensions of divine love and grace. In everything they see, think, and experience, nondualists find the dimensions of the other).

As you read I say, "Welcome to my world! I don't have all the answers, but I believe I ask many of the right questions." As my mantra, I adhere to the principle, "To go deep in any one place is to meet the infinite aliveness that is God, for God is everywhere." Those words provide the clue to the title of this book, for true spirituality is "heart to heart"; such spirituality is the way of nature, of humans, and of God. These three stories are ultimately one story, for all things begin and end in God, in whom "we live and move and have our being" (Acts 17:28).

In the ancient world, wisdom was summed up in the phrase "Know Thyself," words carved into the lintel of the temple of Apollo at Delphi, the sacred sanctuary considered the center of the known world, the place on earth where humans were closest to the gods. There is, however, only one journey: the journeys inward and outward are the journey Godward.

Heart to Heart is written for those who affirm the value of lifelong spiritual growth, realize the limits of logic, and embrace the paradoxes in life. Such people see life as a mystery and often return to sacred stories and symbols, though without being confined to a theological box. This phase of spirituality, identified by James Fowler in his *Stages of Faith* as "conjunctive faith," is often discovered or reached in midlife, though sooner by some. If you are prepared to grow spiritually, morally, and intellectually, I encourage you to embark upon the journey promoted in these two volumes.

Introduction

Entry 1: Overview

Spirituality is universal and timeless. The first humans—our earliest ancestors—were deeply spiritual, and human beings have been spiritual ever since. While we sometimes tend to think of the first humans as primitive—they were certainly primitive technologically—it is better to call them primal, for they came first, and their worldview was more sophisticated than that of many moderns. Everything for them was religious, for they thought of nature as imbued with sanctity. Furthermore, they viewed life and nature with wonder and reverence, for they envisioned no line separating the visible world from the more real spiritual world that surrounds and nurtures the physical realm. Primal peoples were concerned (and continue doing so, for their holistic views are perpetuated in primal societies still found across the globe, such as in Native American groups and societies found throughout North and South America) with the maintenance of personal, social, and cosmic harmony, because for them all things are related.

Primal people are embedded in their world. Their rituals are not attempts to stand apart from or to control nature, for primal people view humanity and nature as belonging to a single order. Rather than attempting to produce extraordinary effects or control nature magically, primal rites focus on maintaining the patterns of nature; they are rituals of cooperation rather than of coercion or manipulation. While articulating basic human needs, these rituals also sustain confidence in the processes of nature, spiritually conceived, and renew hope for the future.

Spiritual and theological understanding, particularly in Western Christianity, can be said to have evolved or progressed through various stages:

1. Primal spirituality (primarily focused on cosmic and holistic spiritual experience, corporately and individually applied). This stage is pre-Christian.

2. Organized religion (primarily focused on scriptures, rituals, dogmas, and clerical intermediaries and on the spiritual experiences they engender). This stage includes classical Judaism and Christianity.

3. Enlightened religious movements (primarily focused on individuals who value rationality and the scientific method). This phase occurred to some extent in medieval scholasticism and flourished during the Enlightenment.

4. Fundamentalist religious movements (primarily a reactionary approach to the rationalistic and scientific advances of the Enlightenment, while valuing its own perceived rationality). This phase flourished in the nineteenth and twentieth centuries.

5. Postmodern spirituality (primarily focused on holistic spiritual experience, corporately and individually applied, based on global and pluralistic values). This stage began in the twentieth century and will be a predominant Western form of spirituality in the twenty-first century.

This progression can be summarized in the following manner: In the beginning a form of spirituality existed that was natural, holistic, and focused on achieving harmony with the universe. That primal spirituality became formalized in religious traditions, under the guidance of prophets, priests and other religious intermediaries. Religious authorities established scriptures and rituals, using rational principles and insights currently in vogue to formulate dogmas and creeds, which became part of the ongoing tradition. Scripture, creeds, and doctrine further shaped spiritual experience. Over time, free-thinking individuals and their followers questioned the methodology and conclusions of organized religion. They began to embrace new spiritual principles valued by progressive people of their time. In the twenty-first century, such values came to include freedom of conscience, reverence for nature, respect for life, compassion for all, non-violence, equality under the law, appreciation of spiritual diversity, openness to new revelation, and the abolition of discrimination based on race, color, sex, religion, age, class, or nationality.

Such spirituality, reinforced by organized religion, has the potential to lead humanity into spiritual enlightenment. While not all evolution, spiritual or psychological, biological or political, is progressive, authentic spirituality seeks the trajectory of an upward spiral.

Entry 2: The Human Identity

Occasionally, in conversation with adults on matters of faith and spirituality, I encounter someone who tells me, "I am Buddhist," or "I am Daoist." At first I am intrigued, because they are not ready to worship with Daoists or join a Sangha (Buddhist monastic community). More recently, I sense that they seem to be using the concepts of Daoism or Buddhism as code words for a progressive or newly found spirituality. Daoism, as taught by its original practitioners, and Buddhism, as taught by the Buddha, are remarkably holistic traditions, building on solid first half of life principles designed to lead to second half of life spirituality.

What does it mean to be human? We ask. What makes a person unique? Does biology have priority? Are personality and spirituality equally significant factors? What about race, gender, and social class? To what extent are we shaped by our upbringing or education, by our friends and loved ones? What roles do our jobs and accomplishments play in our self-image and identity?

When our Western forebears thought of personhood, they searched the realm of art and drama for guidance, settling on the term "person" as definitive. The word "person" comes from the Latin word for "mask" or for the actor's role in a drama. The Judeo-Christian tradition builds on this idea, viewing human personhood as an organic participation in the one personhood that is God. In other words, the human self has no meaning or substance apart from the Selfhood of God. God's personhood, however, is not a mask, but the face behind all masks. We humans are the masks of God, and we play out God's image in myriad ways.

The problem we face in a secular society is that we do not know we are the masks of God. Hence, we are compelled to create our own significance, our own masks and personhood. This makes us—like atoms— inherently unstable. When we do not see our lives as a participation in Another, we are forced to manufacture our own private significance. Needing a word for this phenomenon, modern psychology chose the Latin word for "I," or "ego." This is the atomized self (the small or false self), which does not really "exist" at all. In such a state of insecurity, it overly defends and overly defines itself. This imperial ego becomes the basis for all illusion and evil. It is Adam and Eve trying to survive outside of the Garden, something they cannot do.

Entry 3: Impoverishment of Soul

It is no secret that our world is in a state of crisis. The prognosis is bleak and the conditions may be irreversible. The tip of the iceberg, evident to almost everyone nowadays, is the environmental fate of our entire planet. During the second half of the twentieth century we learned that deterioration in the quality of the air we breathe, the water we drink, and the soil in which we grow our crops seriously threatens our continued life and well-being on this earth.

In addition to environmental degradation and anticipated ecological factors such as unpredictable weather patterns, increasing number and severity of storms, and sea-level rise, we can add pandemics and the outbreak of new diseases, species extinction, malnutrition and widespread famine, terrorism, violence and crime, the breakdown of the family, increased addictive behavior, unemployment, corporate scandals, an increasing income gap between rich and poor, religious fanaticism and sectarian wars, and the list goes on and on.

The current crisis involves many factors: ecological, political, economic, sociological, and ethical. At its core, however, the problem is spiritual. The crisis of spirit, dubbed "the impoverishment of soul" by Matthew Fox, one of today's leading spiritual teachers, is particularly evident in our Western civilization today. Modern societies are characterized by imbalance, or more accurately, by dissociation between the spiritual and physical realms of life.

Ecotheologian Thomas Berry believes our situation today as an earth community is so desperate that we must dream the way forward. We must summon, from our unconscious, ways of seeing with which we are unfamiliar, visions that emerge from deeper within us than our conscious rational minds. As John Philip Newell suggests, reconnecting with our inner depths "will demand a fresh releasing within us of the world of dreams, myths, and the imagination. Whether as individuals or collectively as nations and religious traditions, new beginnings will be born among us when we open to the world of what we do not yet know or what we have forgotten deep within."[1]

1. Newell, *Rebirthing of God*, 89.

Whether the current crisis is curable is debatable, but it clearly requires massive cultural reorientation. More importantly, it requires a transformation of the human spirit and a commitment of will. Only a relationship of genuine harmony with nature and a love of nature's God can transform humans from consumers to caretakers. When historians look back at the start of the twenty-first century, it is hoped that they might remember it most for two commitments: as a time when the peoples of the world made a profound commitment to one another and made an equal commitment to nature. It is thus that we demonstrate our love for God. This book is about spirituality, itself primarily an expression of the human longing for—and our dependence upon—God. This innate sense of dependence on God, explored by many of the personalities we examine in this study, is well summarized by Augustine's famous assertion, "You have made us for yourself, O Lord, and our heart is restless until it rests in you."

In this regard, the most outstanding of the medieval Jewish rationalist philosophers and codifiers of Torah, Maimonides (1135–1204), sees the intellectual love of God as the ultimate aim of religious observance. In his *Mishneh Torah* (Code of the Law), he compares love of God to romantic lovesickness, arguing that humans should pine for God's love constantly. This, he believes, is the true meaning of the phrase "for I am faint with love" in Song of Solomon 2:5, viewing the whole of the Song as a parable to illustrate this theme. In this regard, he views the entirety of nature, meaning the *physical* universe, as God's garment that, while concealing God, also reveals God's glory. This idea is not pantheistic, but rather panentheistic, that all is *in* God.

Entry 4: The Path of Spirituality

Human existence is filled with mental and emotional tension, much of it caused by conflict and polarity. In fact, one cannot live without conflict, and the secret of life is learning to embrace and somehow reconcile one's polarities. To do so successfully requires spirituality. Without spirituality, human beings find themselves trapped in cycles of boredom, irritation, and discontent. By spirituality, I don't mean religion, though they are related.

In the past, people of faith rarely distinguished between being religious and being spiritual. Actually, they rarely used the terms "spiritual" or "spirituality," collapsing them under the broader category of religion. What we call spirituality today they might have called "piety," analogous to "being religious." Today, the terms "spiritual" and "spirituality" are in vogue, as opposed to the term" religious," which, like "piety," is often used negatively or pejoratively as a synonym for "religiosity."

While we can define religion or theology with some degree of meaning and specificity, the word "spirituality" is often used traditionally with little or no clear meaning, or in a broad and vague manner. In antiquity, the word was not used, and when first introduced in the English-speaking world, it referred to the clergy, specifically to the ecclesiastical vocation, as distinct from secular or temporal vocations. From this sixteenth-century usage, the term came to describe spiritual as distinct from material things, including spirits, ghosts, or souls.

The meaning of a religious way of life, notably one's piety or acts of religious devotion, came still later, although its use in Ignatius Loyola's *Spiritual Exercises* referred to the practice of piety and more specifically, techniques of devotion. When first used in the French-speaking world, the term "spirituality" was a term of reproach, associated with mystical or ascetic devotion such as used by pietists and related sects and movements not in the religious mainstream. In this respect, spirituality represented an excess of striving after the purely immaterial.

By the nineteenth century, the term was no longer one of reproach but simply a description of prayerful piety, with a view toward the practice of ascetics and mystics. At times spirituality came to be associated with the "inner" or "interior life" of humans in general. In the first half of the twentieth century, the terms spirituality and spiritual theology were applied to ascetic and mystical theology, as opposed to dogmatic and moral theology.

In the nineteenth and twentieth centuries, with the advance of biblical criticism and widespread skepticism on matters of faith, pious people focused on religious practice (*lex orandi*) over against the vicissitudes of historical belief (*lex credenti*), and "spirituality" expressed what was sought. In the late twentieth century, the word "spirituality" found wide usage yet went undefined, having a vague association with living holistically, contemplatively, fully, and harmoniously with nature, others, and all of life. This latter perspective, that all life has a spiritual aspect, is associated widely with spirituality, and the term has become disengaged from theology in general or religion in particular.

Such lack of specificity, however, makes the concept so universal as to lack value. For our purposes, I reconnect the term with its root meaning, that is, with Spirit, or as the ancient Hebrews did, with the "wind" or "breath" of God. To be spiritual is to breathe deeply and harmoniously with Reality (Infinity). Spirituality, then, is a hopeful, creative, life-filled path, a Spirit-filled way of living. Taking a path is a different way of living from driving down a highway. Unlike highways, paths seem more personal. Unlike a highway, paths are not goal-oriented, for spirituality implies choice, uncertainty, and risk-taking. To quote Matthew Fox, one of today's leading spiritual teachers, spirituality is

> the way itself, and every moment on the way is a holy moment; a sacred seeing takes place there. All who embark on a spiritual path need to be willing to learn and to let go; to know that none of us has all the answers, and yet that none of us is apart from deity. . . What is common to all paths that are spiritual is, of course, the Spirit—breath, life, energy. That is why all true paths are essentially one path—because there is only one Spirit, one breath, one life, one energy in the universe. It belongs to none of us and all of us. We all share it. Spirituality does not make us otherworldly; it renders us more fully alive. The path that spirituality takes is a path away from the superficial into the depths; away from the "outer person" into the "inner person"; away from the privatized and individualistic into the deeply communitarian.[2]

Spirituality, traditionally defined by Christians as "life in the Spirit," encompasses the journey of life from a distinct perspective. Spirituality is the journey of life "from God, to God, and with God." As a result, it is also a journey toward self. In other words, the process of coming to know or to experience God is also the process of knowing oneself. Through this process, one comes to differentiate between one's temporary or false self, which we call the ego, and one's permanent or True Self, that part of us made in the image of God and made for ongoing or everlasting relationship with God. In the end, we discover that we know God by being known, much like one loves by being loved.

Thinking comprehensively, then, spirituality involves what is, what can be, and what ought to be. When activity, rationality, and morality are infused with creativity and imagination, meaning that when body, mind, and soul are inspired or harmonious with Spirit (that is, inspired, infused and energized by Spirit), spirituality is authentic, healthy, and vital.

---

2. Fox, *Creation Spirituality*, 12.

Entry 5: The Task at Hand

While *Heart to Heart* discusses religious and theological issues, particularly from a progressive Christian perspective, our focus is on spirituality. This book is not a handbook on spirituality, not a step-by-step instruction manual on how to be more spiritual, for spirituality is the journey of a lifetime. While spirituality requires effort, it is also effortless, in that it requires letting go. In the journey of spirituality, progress is expected; there are steps forward, certainly, but also many more backward. The goal of spirituality is always God, and while God makes the journey interesting, it is never easy. Orthodox or traditional spirituality—what we call first half of life spirituality—is formulaic and instructional; in other words, it can be taught. Second half of life spirituality is more caught than taught, for there are no clear steps to follow or learn. This book, while dealing with orthodox Christianity's struggle for supremacy, focuses on rebels and free thinkers, on those who may not necessarily have reached their goal of union with God but come to understand that somehow the journey is the goal.

The central defining characteristic of spirituality is an individual's sense of connection to a greater whole. At its heart, spirituality involves an emotional experience of awe and reverence. Such experience is highly desired, fervently sought, endlessly disagreed upon, and thoroughly fascinating. Why did our ancestors have such a wonderful idea of God? Because they lived in an awesome world. They wondered at the magnificence of whatever it was that brought the world into being. This led to a sense of adoration. This adoration, this gratitude, we call religion. Now, as the outer world is diminished, our inner world is drying up. The task of spirituality is to help us regain our sense of awe and reverence, beginning with a profound commitment to nature and continuing with an equal commitment to the whole of humanity and every living creature. If we do not love what is visible around us, how can we love God, whom we cannot see? (1 John 4:19–20).

As you read this book, you will undoubtedly come across ideas with which you may disagree, ideas you will accept wholeheartedly, and ideas you have never heard before, ideas that may keep you thinking late into the night. Expect to be challenged, perplexed, and frustrated, but also to grow spiritually and intellectually in ways you never imagined.

The Phenomenon of Religion

Entry 1: The Role of Religion

THE PHENOMENON OF RELIGION has been pervasive throughout the history of humanity and continues to be central to most cultures of the world. The role of religion in the current clash between cultures, whether viewed through a secular, traditional, or fundamentalist lens, is enormous, and any headway we are able to make in the future in terms of peace and international cooperation will involve moral principles that value and encourage ecumenical understanding and inter-religious dialogue.

The role of religion, whether in formulating a worldview or in shaping a lifestyle, has until recently been considered indispensable. Religion is one of several systems devised by humans to provide guidance and meaning to the whole order of existence. The original role of religion was not divisive but holistic. It was not about creating polarities, institutions, hierarchies, or doctrines. Rather, the original role of religion was to promote harmonious spirituality.

In his 1962 book, *The Meaning and End of Religion*, Harvard professor of comparative religion Wilfred Cantwell Smith noted the difference in meaning of the contemporary concept of "religion," a relatively recent invention in European history, and the original meaning of the term. Christian writers began using the term "religion" during the seventeenth century to signify a system of ideas or beliefs about God. But that is not the original meaning of the word religion or of its Latin root *religio*. Unlike religion as a system of belief, *religio* signified the awe that human beings felt in the presence of the unknown. It included a response to a subjective experience, an attitude of trust and reverence toward the divine or toward nature. As something within one's heart, *religio* involved a path of wonder through the wilderness of change and uncertainty. For Smith, what is ending and what needs to end is the modern Western understanding of religion, not its original subjective, intuitive, passionate dimension.

What we have seen in recent times, not only in the West but also globally, is a turning from religion and a return to *religio*, only it is being called "spirituality," since no other English term conveys the new religious sensibility. In the past, people of faith rarely distinguished between being religious and being spiritual. Actually, they rarely used the terms "spiritual" or "spirituality," collapsing them under the broader category of religion. What we call spirituality today they might have called "piety," analogous to "being religious." Today, the terms "spiritual" and "spirituality" are in vogue, as opposed to the term" religious," which, like "piety," is often used negatively or pejoratively as a synonym for "religiosity."

In recent studies, religious pollsters in a number of countries have begun asking people whether they consider themselves "spiritual but *not* religious; religious but *not* spiritual; religious *and* spiritual; or *not* spiritual and *not* religious." The most surprising result is to the first option. In the United States, 30 percent of adults declared they were "spiritual but not religious." In Canada, 40 percent selected this choice, and in England, as many as 51 percent understood themselves in this way. In 2009, Princeton Survey Research Associates found that only 9 percent of Americans considered themselves "religious but not spiritual," while some 48 percent viewed themselves as "religious and spiritual." The World Values Survey, associated with the University of Michigan, found that in many developed nations, as high as 70 percent of the population self-defined as "generalized spirituality in contrast to traditional religions."[1] As these polls demonstrate, the word "spiritual" is far more appealing in post-Christian societies than the term "religious."

In *Christianity After Religion*, American theologian Diana Bass notes that for much of Western history, the words "religious" and "spiritual" meant roughly the same thing, namely, how humans relate with God through rituals, practices, and communal worship. However, the popular meaning of the words diverged during the twentieth century. The word "spiritual" gradually came to be associated with the private realm of thought and experience, while the word "religious" came to be connected with the public realm of membership in religious institutions, participation in formal ritual, and adherence to official denominational doctrines. In general, "spirituality" came

---

1. Bass, *Christianity After Religion*, 66.

to take a positive and attractive meaning, as somehow authentic, whereas "religious" took on a more negative connotation.

Entry 2: Primal Religion

The first humans were animists; they were conscious that nature was spirit-infused. Their life was holistic; individuals and groups alike viewed the natural, social, and spiritual dimensions as profoundly integrated. Primal cultures—that is, tribes or communities having no scriptures, literate sources of guidance, or linear sense of history—represent primitive attempts to establish harmony with the powers such groups sensed directing human life. Spirituality, for primal peoples, means direct relationship between human beings and the deeper realm around and within them, which they view as more powerful and real than the realm they experience through the senses. While we cannot speak of primal religious systems in the singular, whether in Asia, Australia, Africa, or America, nonetheless, there are sufficient common or similar elements in these to speak of each region in a collective singular.

To understand primal cultures, a good place to begin is with their sense of embeddedness. This starts with the tribe, apart from which there is little independent identity. Through the tribe, individuals participate with nature in a unified order. Despite the cultural variety represented by these traditions, three common patterns are evident in their spirituality: (1) the solidarity of human beings with the natural world, (2) the centering of individual human existence in the social community, and (3) the reciprocity of the human spirit with the world of spirits transcending the human. Significantly, each of these holds together elements of reality that have undergone systematic alienation in Western culture.

In the Greco-Roman world, there were many religions, including Judaism and Christianity. In the Roman Empire, religion was prominent in society, and virtually everyone was religious. It was rare for anyone to be atheistic. Pagans were clearly religious, as everyone accepted the existence of the gods. Not everyone worshiped the gods, but all accepted their existence. Religion was needed, people agreed, because they knew they were powerless over the forces of life that could harm them. As mortals, they knew they were limited in their ability, unable to control such things as drought, war, or disease. They knew there were matters even in their own personal lives that were beyond their control, such as whether their children would be healthy, their spouses remain loyal, or their crops grow. Religion was a way of getting what they couldn't provide for themselves. In other words, people needed someone more powerful than themselves, a role fulfilled by the gods.

Ancient religions were almost entirely polytheistic. Prior to the emergence of Christianity and Islam, the only exception was Judaism. Everyone else in the Roman world worshiped many gods, for their gods were not sovereign, omnipotent, or exclusive. Each god had a role, controlling some aspect of human life. There were national gods; gods of localities (each city had its own god); gods of places (such as of rivers, meadows, and forests); gods over every function (such as of one's home, of the pantry, and of the hearth; gods of crops, of healing and rain, of childbirth, and so forth).

Religion in the ancient world was a way of worshiping these forces, a way of currying favor with benevolent deities while avoiding offending their capricious nature. Worship involved the performance of cultic acts such as performing sacrifices on their behalf and offering prayers as a sign of humility and submission. The root of the word "cultic" in the sense of devotion comes from the Latin phrase *cultus deorum*, meaning "care of the gods." The gods, like humans, had needs, and devotees took care of the gods in order that the gods might take care of their needs. Worship, in this sense, was mutually beneficial. Humans felt the gods' needs could be met through sacrifices, preferably by offering animals or things that were grown, items valuable to humans as well. Sacrifices could be offered in one's home, preferably before one's meals, in the form of a libation poured out or as a burnt offering on a family altar. Larger or more elaborate sacrifices, such as that of animals, were conducted in public temples, many of these places of gathering and worship led by priests and other officials appointed by local authorities to serve as intermediaries with the gods.

Each locale and region had its religious festivals, which citizens and residents of communities sponsored for public well-being. Festivals often celebrated the birthdate of a god or commemorated beneficent deeds on the part of the local or national deity. Many of these festivals were sponsored by the state. In addition to state religions, each region and town had its own god, and it was common for each family to have a preferred god or goddess.

Entry 3: Ancient Pagan Religion

What is common to pagan religions is the absence of beliefs. Believing specific things about the gods was not significant to personal religion. What mattered was that the needs of the gods be met through cultic sacrifice and prayer. It was necessary that one believe in the existence of the gods, of course, and in the obligation of sacrifice, but beliefs about specific aspects of the gods, such as their nature, their demands, or what they wanted devotees to believe about them, these were private matters, unessential to worship and practice. Such things might be relevant to mythology—the stories about the gods—or matters for philosophers to discuss or debate, but they were irrelevant to personal religion.

As odd as it might seem to us, ancient Greek and Roman religions had no beliefs to affirm, theologies to embrace, or creeds to recite. When people went to the temples, they performed sacrifices. They did not recite creeds or confess theological beliefs. As a result, in all religions of the Greco-Roman age, there was no such thing as heresy or orthodoxy, because there was no insistence on right belief or criticism of wrong belief, only an emphasis on the cultic acts necessary to appease the gods. Interestingly, there were no ethical standards associated with these religions. Religions did not establish particular rules of morality. Although the gods were offended by such acts as patricide, they seemed unconcerned with misbehavior such as adultery or cheating on taxes. Such deeds did not disqualify one from worship. Even the gods were known to behave immorally or hypocritically. Such things mattered philosophically, but they were not issues that concerned the gods.

The one exception to matters of behavior and belief in the ancient world was Judaism. Judaism emphasized specific beliefs, such as belief in the one true God who called Israel to be his people and instructed them how to live in community and to worship him alone. However, Judaism was a minority religion, comprising about 7 percent of the population during the period of the Roman Empire. Furthermore, the Jews did not condemn Gentiles for worshiping many gods. Their God had chosen them, and they in response had chosen to worship their God alone. Through much of their history to this point, the Jews were henotheists, worshiping one God among many. Others could choose to worship different gods, but God was the god they had chosen, and their loyalty and worship was to their God alone. This God had given them a scripture—the Torah—a set of sacred books with laws only they were obligated to keep. Greco-Roman religions did not have sacred books—they were not scripturally based, as were Judaism and Christianity.

Christianity began as a sect within Judaism. Unlike other religions, including Judaism, Christianity was, from the outset, a religion that emphasized belief. It stressed that Jews, along with all other unbelievers, needed to believe that Jesus was the Messiah, God's long-awaited redeemer who would save believers from their sins. We see this belief in Jesus as Redeemer already in the earliest Christian sources, the letters of Paul, written between twenty to thirty years after Jesus' death, well before the appearance of the first gospels. In his letters, Paul indicates that Jesus is the fulfillment of the written scriptures of the Jews. For Paul, belief in Jesus is essential, the only way to be right with God.

From the beginning, then, Christianity was structured as a religion that de-emphasized cultic acts such as sacrifice and emphasized proper belief. Christians did not perform sacrifices to their God because they believed Jesus was the perfect and complete sacrifice. Their religion was based on accepting the sacrifice of Jesus on their behalf, rather than on performing sacrifices on his behalf. In this respect, Christianity was a religion of belief rather than of cultic act.

Moreover, unlike other religions of the Greek and Roman period, Christianity was exclusivistic. No other religion—perhaps excepting Judaism, although, as we shall see, ancient Judaism was not as exclusivistic as we might think—insisted that to worship their god, you could not worship other gods. Ancient religions were inclusivistic, accepting one another. If someone decided to worship a new god, such as when one moved to a new town and wished to adopt its deity, that didn't require giving up one's former god or gods. Many gods were believed to exist, all desiring worship. Christianity, however, claimed that the only way to be right with God was through belief in Jesus. This teaching made other religions wrong, and Christianity right. Faith or belief in Jesus made Christianity unique in the ancient world, its missionary consciousness contributing to its expansion and widespread growth.

This emphasis on belief also brought Christianity into contact with pagan philosophical schools prevalent in Greco-Roman culture. Many educated Christians, together with certain Hellenized Jews, engaged philosophically with their pagan counterparts, intellectualizing and mythologizing their belief system to make it more accessible, attractive, and compatible with philosophical tradition. The emphasis on exclusivism, however, exaggerated the need for proto-orthodox Christians to be correct in what they believed, adhering more literally to the developing apostolic tradition, refining what it meant to believe in Jesus. As a result, they felt they had to be precise about Jesus, who he was and what he taught, and what Christians needed to believe if they were to be right with God. If salvation depended upon belief, Christianity needed to clarify what had to be believed. As it turned out, different opinions emerged as to who Jesus was and what it meant to believe in him. Different theologies, christologies, and soteriologies developed and came to be embraced. Controversies ensued and soon creeds came into being, different Christian groups affirming different beliefs.

Each group needed its own authority for what it believed, and each claimed that its beliefs were rooted in the teachings of Jesus' apostles and, through them, to Jesus himself. In particular, each group stressed that its authority was based on its own sacred writings, allegedly produced by one or more apostles of Jesus. Distinct groups emerged, favoring certain writings over others.

Entry 4: Religion as Noun or Adjective

If religion is central to culture, there should be agreement among scholars on a definition of religion, but no consensus exists. In order to provide distinction between religion and non-religion, some scholars appeal to a distinction between two realms of reality, the sacred and the secular, arguing that human involvement with the sacred defines the essence of religion.

The notion that religion can be defined as human interaction with the sacred has a long legacy in the West. This view, based upon a sacred-secular dualism, divides the world into two domains, the one containing all that is sacred and the other all that is profane. This understanding of religion was advanced and popularized in the middle of the twentieth century in Mircea Eliade's classic work *The Sacred and the Profane: The Nature of Religion*.

This distinction, based on an antiquated dualistic perspective long entrenched in the Western mindset, provides insuperable problems for many modern individuals, whose experience leads them to conceptualize the sacred (and therefore the supernatural, the spiritual, the metaphysical, and the nonmaterial) as a projection and/or an extension of society, thereby collapsing the sacred into the profane (the natural, physical, and material). This approach, while appearing reductionist, need not be dismissive of the sacred as a purely human construct. The intention can be cautionary about the inherent problems with the sacred-profane dualism and instructive in noting that this dualistic worldview is not a universal idea but a particularly Western (and monotheistic) construction.[2]

John Esposito, longtime professor and author of texts on world religions, highlights the difficulty of defining the term "religion" by asking his readers to engage in a thought experiment.[3] Suppose you could enter a time machine, he suggests, and be transported back to the city of Rome in the first century. He selects ancient Rome because the word "religion" has its roots in the Latin language of the Roman Empire, and also because understanding how the Romans used the word might help us define what we mean by the term religion today.

Imagine that you are walking down a street in ancient Rome, and you approach a group of people standing on a corner. You ask: "What religion are you?" but they seem puzzled by the question. They understand the individual words, but the phrasing seems awkward and they do not understand what you are asking. So you rephrase the question: "Are you religious?" This causes them to smile and reply, "Of course, isn't everyone?"

Why did they understand the second question but not the first? According to Esposito, the first question treats the word religion as a noun describing distinct social bodies, such that each person understands himself or herself as identifying with and belonging to only one of those organization; if you are a Christian, you are by definition not a Jew or a Buddhist. But this way of understanding would be foreign to a person living in antiquity, and today it is foreign to many people living in Africa and Asia. Esposito points out that in Japan even today it is possible to be Buddhist, Daoist, Confucian, and Shinto all at the same time.

Once you rephrase the question from "What religion are you?" to "Are you religious?" you shift the function of the term religion from being a noun describing a distinct social group to being an adjective describing "an attitude toward the human condition—a way of seeing, acting, and experiencing all things."[4] According to Esposito, throughout history most people

---

2. Here I have in mind the attitude that dismisses, condemns, reduces, and stereotypes all nonmonotheistic beliefs and practices as "idolatrous," as though reducing all divinity and spirituality to one's own cherished singularity were not itself idolatrous.

3. Esposito, *World Religions Today*, 5–7.

4. Esposito, *World Religions Today*, 6.

did not think of religion as a noun, as a separate reality they had to choose over and against another reality.

Esposito suggests that ancient Greeks and Romans viewed religion as a way of respecting all powers, natural and supernatural, that govern one's destiny, whether they be associated with war, fertility, or other aspects of society. Of course one would want all those forces on one's side. Anything else would be disastrous. For ancient Romans, as for nearly all other people throughout history, religion was essentially about divine favor and its influence on human destiny. According to this perspective, religion is not just about "spiritual" things, or deities, or God. Rather, religious attitudes are as diverse as the forms of power that people believe govern their destiny, whether these forms of power are related to nature, wealth, political power, individual wellbeing, or the forces of history.

Esposito's emphases seem spot-on. He is certainly correct to point out that the contemporary tendency to think of religion as a noun is rather unique to the contemporary Western world and that such a view represents a departure from what has been commonly understood by most people throughout history. Also, Esposito's attempt to reframe religion as an attitude toward power, in which he includes social, political, and economic power, suggests that religion must be understood as a phenomenon pervading all of society, rather than as a distinct element existing in but separate from other elements of society.

Entry 5: Healthy and "Junk" Religion

At their inception, world religions were healthy, wholesome, and beneficial. Over time, particularly as religions became institutionalized, that changed, so much so that we need to distinguish between "healthy" religion and "junk" religion. Healthy religion provides a foundational sense of awe. It re-enchants an otherwise empty universe. It encourages reverence toward all things, enabling people of faith to see the reflection of the divine image in the human, the animal, and the entire natural world, which now become enchanted, that is, inherently supernatural. When humans are fully alert in spirit, mind, and body, their identity transcends their imagination, and they can accomplish more than they suppose. Moments of awareness occur as a dawning of meaning, when the familiar suddenly becomes infused with new insight and possibilities, and when unfamiliar ideas challenge and pervade our consciousness. Such occasions feel like personal discoveries.

Instead of providing awe, reconnection, and awakening, junk religion—on both the left and the right of the religious spectrum—leads to sectarianism, ideological divisiveness, emotionalism, and even social and political hysteria. Similar to junk food because it only satisfies enough to gratify momentary desires, junk religion does not truly feed the intellect or the heart. Junk religion is usually characterized by dependence on the past, often leading to fear of the present as well as of the future. However, when religion leads us to encounter the divine, we are empowered to embrace not only the present but also the future without anxiety or fear. There is no fear of the present because it is viewed as full of potential. There is no fear of the future because a loving God is in charge. In addition, there is no fear of the past because the past has been healed and forgiven.

In authentic religion, people do not use theology to avoid reality or to fabricate a private, self-serving reality. Authentic believers let God lead them into the fullness of Reality—not into delusions, distrust, or conspiracy thinking, and not away from dilemmas, paradoxes, and uncertainties, but directly into the throes of their humanity.

Whatever reconstruction we need to undergo individually and as a society cannot be based on fear or on reaction. It must be based on a positive and fully human experience of God as a loving Presence. Healthy religion is ready to let God be God, and to embrace a future we do not yet understand—and no longer need to understand.

The Spiritual Journey, Part I

Entry 1: The Journey of Faith

ANYONE WHO IS GROWING is on a journey, and anyone growing spiritually is on a faith journey. While some may have difficulty seeing life as a journey of any sort, let alone a journey of faith, everyone needs to get in touch with their own story.

Expanding one's religious outlook, deepening one's relation to the sacred and infinite, is essential for persons to age creatively. Carl Jung (1875–1961), the prominent Swiss psychiatrist, emphasized that gaining a religious attitude, the kind that allows us to see our own personal lives as moving toward wholeness and our own stories as related to a larger story, is the psychological/spiritual task for one's later years: "Among all my patients in the second half of life—that is to say, over thirty-five—there has not been one whose problem in the last resort was not that of finding a religious outlook on life." If Jung was correct, then discovering one's personal way to relate to God and to speak about ultimate concerns may well be the most significant task of life.

American Christians seem always to be on a journey of faith. The priority given to religious faith in America is demonstrated by the great variety of utopian movements and sectarian denominations that have flourished in the North American continent. Among the driving forces in American society has been the manifestation of Christian fervency known as "Great Awakenings." Such revivals punctuate America's historical record, rooting America's hopes in religious traditionalism.

Recent data concerning religious affiliation in America indicate an alarming trend occurring among all Christian denominations: religious affiliation is plummeting. However, such news is not all negative, as it never is in America, for this loss in affiliation is coupled with a rise of interest in "spirituality." The decline in Christian attendance and affiliation that began decades ago—and is increasing exponentially in recent years—has a hopeful side, for it is leading many Christians to approach faith with a newfound freedom both life-giving and service driven. Some are calling this emerging movement a Fourth Great Awakening, finding here a way of faith closer to the real message of Jesus. An unexamined faith, as many Christians are discovering, may not be worth following, since it is not one's own.

The world's great spiritual personalities—Moses, Buddha, the prophets of Israel, Jesus, Muhammad, to name a few—were considered revolutionaries and even heretics in their day. They inspired their early followers to break from tradition and update their relationships to God. On his deathbed the Buddha urged his disciples: "Do not accept what you hear by report, do not accept tradition, do not accept a statement because it is found in our books, nor because it is in accord with your belief, nor because it is the saying of your teacher. Be lamps unto yourselves." It would be difficult to heed the Buddha's sage advice without being on a faith journey.

Entry 2: From Precritical to Postcritical Believer, Part I

Change and growth are intrinsic to life. As humans grow by progressing physically, psychologically, emotionally, and intellectually, so they undergo various stages of growth in their faith. Healthy human beings are said to go through discernible stages of growth throughout their lifetime. According to psychologist Erik Erikson, psychosocial development proceeds by critical steps. Each stage is marked by crisis, connoting not a catastrophe but a turning point, a crucial period of increased vulnerability and heightened potential. At such points, achievements are won or failures occur, leaving the future to some degree better or worse but in any case, restructured.

Most humans, ancient and modern alike, pattern their lives after some model, whether consciously or unconsciously. These models can be cultural, civic, intellectual, historical, cyclical, developmental, religious, or spiritual. Many people follow more than one pattern simultaneously. Most educated people in the West today have little trouble identifying with terms such as premodern, modern, or postmodern. They are also familiar with Karl Marx's adaptation of Hegel's thesis, antithesis, and synthesis as stages of social and economic development. This model has also been used to describe three stages of growth toward citizenship: claiming (thesis), doubting (antithesis), and redeeming (synthesis).

A similar model, consisting of precritical, critical, and postcritical stages, has been applied to theological, existential, and intellectual development. The *precritical phase*, also called precritical naiveté, first naiveté, or first simplicity, is an early state in which children accept whatever significant authority figures in their lives tell them to be true as indeed true. For some this state is short-lived; for others, it can last a lifetime.

In their early teens, some begin to question their beliefs, experiencing a collision between childhood beliefs and those of modernity. In late adolescence, college students often become exposed to the scholarly study of religion, to teachings of religions different from their own, to claims of science, and to atheistic or agnostic professors and points of view. Those who take these views seriously often enter the stage of *critical understanding*, from which there seems to be no way back. Some remain perplexed about God and conclude that there probably is no such reality. This second phase is a critical one, or possibly even an apathetic reaction to the first phase. In this phase, some abandon prayer and stop attending formal worship altogether, living as post-religious inhabitants of the secular city. For many "second phasers," critical reason becomes the object of their faith and secular humanism becomes their creed.

Those who persevere in their faith journey often discover that agnosticism and atheism are more like temporary stops than final destinations. Something happens to them—a mystical experience, something traumatic, a relationship, a sudden realization—and the word "God" becomes meaningful once again, only this time not as a reference to a supernatural being "out there" but to the sacred at the center of existence. God is no longer a mere idea or an article of belief external to oneself but rather an element of experience. Such persons have reached the state of *postcritical understanding* (also called postcritical naiveté, second naiveté, or second simplicity), a state where one participates in religious rituals because they are meaningful and not because they are required, where one hears ancient biblical stories as "true" while knowing them as not literally true.

Those who enter the third phase retain an appreciation of critical reason, but have moved beyond secular humanism in search of sacred ground. Third-phase believers understand their lives as open-ended journeys in which they seek, not an end to ambiguity and uncertainty, but rather breadth, depth, and meaning. They realize that life is a pilgrimage, and that the entire earth can become hallowed ground and therefore the locus of encounter with the living God.

Entry 3: From Precritical to Postcritical Believer, Part II

Perhaps your spiritual experience is similar to mine. You have known about God since your childhood, having been taught that God is loving, gracious, just, forgiving, almighty, and omnipresent. You believe in God, and you would even say you love God. At times your love of God may have been passionate and intense, but overall, more lukewarm or cold than hot. You consider yourself spiritual, and you have practiced the disciplines of devotion such as attending church, reading scripture, meditation, and giving of your time and money to church and to those in need. Your prayer life has been habitual, though mostly limited to mealtime or to situations of anxiety, uncertainty, or perplexity. Although there have been times when you prayed regularly and faithfully, even then God seemed silent and remote.

You long for God, desiring intimacy with this source and ground of your being, yet you feel you do not know God directly. Your religious upbringing taught you a great deal about God, and perhaps you had a conversion experience. There may have been times when you felt God communicating with you or through you—perhaps through a vision, a dream, an insight, or in ways that had no other explanation—yet your desire for intimacy with God went unfulfilled. In the end, however, all of these seem somehow unconvincing, for the impulse, initiative, and motivation appeared more human than divine. You desire something more, and are unsure that all this spiritual activity is but a human contrivance, a way of meeting some human need for meaning and transcendence.

The apostle Paul was commenting on human spirituality in general when he noted that "we see through a glass, darkly" (1 Cor 13:12, KJV). Yet inadequate vision of the divine need not prevent us from occasional glimpses of light in the darkness. While the human experience often takes us into great deserts of doubt, dryness, and lostness, we need not remain there. How often we see only our failures and forget those times when we have been channels of divine love.

While many seekers today choose to remain in this critical phase, perplexed by the competing views promoted by multicultural traditions, world religions, and by secular worldviews, those who persevere in their faith journey discover that agnosticism and atheism are not final destinations but rather temporary stops.

Speaking as a postcritical Christian, I am heartened by the words of Morton Kelsey, a counselor, spiritual director, and therapist who reflected on his own agnostic phase when he wrote: "To help the questioning, the agnostic and the atheist, [spiritual counselors] need to be people who have struggled with doubt themselves and have come out on the other side with a meaningful faith. . . . The trouble with most people is that they are not agnostic enough; they are not consistent in their agnosticism and do not go into it far enough to see its darkness and agony."[1]

In a letter to one he was guiding, Abbé Huvelin, one of the most accomplished spiritual directors of all times, spoke from personal experience when he wrote: "In faith we have just enough light to follow the right way, but on either side there is an abyss." The abyss of agnosticism, manifested in cosmic rootlessness, can cause unbelievable pain and suffering, as we learn from the writings of atheistic existentialists such as Sartre and Camus. Feeling alone in a meaningless world, however, often results in more than existentialist despair. It has emotional and physical consequences as well.

In his autobiography, *Memories, Dreams, Reflections* (1963), and in earlier works such as *Modern Man in Search of a Soul* (1933), Carl Jung tells how he was jolted from the rational, materialistic agnosticism of his medical training. A colleague of Freud, he broke with Freud after discovering there was a nonphysical dimension or reality, observable to anyone who would take the trouble to experience it. It was, he said, as experienceable as were the two moons of Jupiter to those in Galileo's time who were willing to look through his telescope. Jung believed that one of his most important therapeutic tasks was to free people trapped in the constricting materialistic outlook of modernity and to open them up to a more adequate view of reality. He viewed the person caught up in materialism as more sick than amoral or immoral.

One of Jung's important contributions to modern psychology and theology was his recognition that the inability to believe in anything, or the belief in a meaningless world, could be classified as disease or sickness and could cause as much damage as childhood trauma, acute tension, or a dose of poison. Believing that one has no meaningful place in the universe is not only a disease or sickness, but it can result in actual emotional and physical illness. Numerous devastating emotions may result from the

1. Kelsey, *Companions on the Inner Way*, 61.

sense of living in a hostile or indifferent universe, ranging from fear, anger, and stress to loneliness and depression. Studies show that 60 percent of those under continuous stress actually suffer some serious physical illness within twelve to eighteen months.

Much of the drug dependency of our time is surely related to the psychic sense of meaninglessness in the universe, coupled with the fear that no one loves and accepts us as we are. From this perspective, life seems unfair, particularly if it ends with extinction at death. When there is no friendliness in the universe, there is little reason to expect it from other human beings, and less reason to reach out to others. Our separation from social meaning can lead to isolation, loneliness, and depression, which makes us susceptible to contamination by the fear, anger, depression, stress, and hopelessness of others. Psychic infection usually strikes below the conscious level and is difficult to deal with consciously. Rebuilding seems hopeless, and people tend to give up on life, inwardly and outwardly. How can human beings overcome inner anxiety and rage without a sense of purpose and the hope of some meaning in this world and beyond?

One of the functions of the church is to provide a decompression chamber into which we can step out of the negativity and hopelessness so rampant in our society. However, when the church fails to offer an environment of love, meaning, and concern, both human and transhuman, and when it becomes caught up in its own survival, reflecting the fears and suspicions of its weakest members, has it not lost its way? If salt loses its savor, has it any value?

Entry 4: The Second Journey, Part I

Of the many models regarding spirituality, one I find compelling is known as the "second half of life." This "further journey" is not chronological, nor does one magically stumble upon it at midlife or in times of crisis, though these often serve as catalysts. While the second journey represents the culmination of one's faith journey, it is largely unknown today, even by people we consider deeply religious, since most individuals and institutions remain stymied in the preoccupations of the first half of life, establishing identity, creating boundary markers, and seeking security. The first half of life task, while essential, is not the full journey. Furthermore, one cannot walk the second journey with first-journey tools. One needs a new toolkit.

The first task is to build a strong "container" or identity; the second is to find the contents that the container is meant to hold.[2] The first task—surviving successfully—is obvious, one we take for granted as the purpose of life. We all want to complete successfully the task that life first hands us: establishing an identity, a home, a career, relationships, friends, community, and security, all foundational for getting started in life. Many cultures throughout history, most empires in antiquity, and the majority of individuals in the modern period have focused on first half of life tasks, primarily because it is all they have time for, but also for lack of vision.

Most of us are never told that we can set out from the known and the familiar to take on a further journey. Our institutions, including our churches, are almost entirely configured to encourage, support, reward, and validate the tasks of the first half of life. Shocking and disappointing as it may be, we struggle more to survive than to thrive, focusing on "getting through" or on getting ahead rather than on finding out what is at the top or was already at the bottom. As wilderness guide Bill Plotkin puts it, many of us learn to do our "survival dance," but we never get to our actual "sacred dance."

According to Plotkin, the stage of adolescence—beyond which most adults never move—holds the key to both individual development and human evolution. In this stage individuals develop their distinctive ego-based consciousness, which represents both their greatest liability as well as their greatest potential. If they are to become fully human and move to the stages of genuine adulthood, people in the adolescent stage must let go of the familiar and comfortable while submitting to a journey of descent into "the mysteries of nature and the human soul." Individuals who remain within the constraints of a largely adolescent world regress into "pathological adolescence," characterized by materialism, sexism, competitive violence, racism, egoism, and self-destructive patterns. Patho-adolescent societies are perpetuated by leaders and celebrities described as self-serving politicians, moralizing religious leaders, drug-induced entertainment icons, and greedy captains of industry. If society is going to develop soulcentrically, it must be overseen by wise elders, not by adolescent politicians and corporate officers.

How can we know we are entering the second half of life? The following road markers are quite reliable: when we

2. Rohr, *Falling Upward*, xiii.

- experience new urges

- sense a new vision

- are ready to let go of old securities

- are ready to risk giving up the patterns of the past
  for the promise of the future

- are as focused on the "inner" life as on
  the outer dimension of life

While individuals can describe their experience of the second journey and even serve as mentors, they cannot define or outline the journey for others. This is due both to the uniqueness of the journey and to a subtle factor, known by generations of mystics and spiritual masters but elusive to many of our contemporaries: we do not choose this second journey; rather it chooses us. It finds us by means of our soul, our personal center and true home, the source of our true belonging. The soul comes to our aid through dreams, deep emotion, love, the quiet voice of guidance, synchronicities, revelations, hunches, and visions, and at times through illness, nightmares, and terrors. This identity defines us, aligning us with our powers of nurturing, transforming, and creating, and with our sense of presence and wonder. The soul guides us, preparing the way and declaring us ready for this further journey.

If we haven't acquired conscious knowledge of our soul, we haven't yet learned of its power. To experience this power, which serves as a bridge to the second half of life, we must first get to know more thoroughly the place in life we already inhabit. This place consists of our relationships and roles in both society and nature. We achieve this knowledge and intimacy through the practice of mindfulness, learning to dwell deeply in the present moment.

In this second half of life, we are less interested in judging or punishing others, or in harboring superiority complexes. By now these things have shown themselves to be useless, ego-based, and counterproductive. Daily life now requires discernment more than kneejerk response toward either the conservative or liberal end of the spectrum. In the second half of life we focus less on commandments and precepts and more on changing our attitude, on forgiving others rather than criticizing or finding fault.

Life is more spacious now, the boundaries of our lives having been enlarged by the addition of new experiences and relationships. This may be what Ken Wilber means when he says "the classic spiritual journey always begins elitist and ends egalitarian." In the second half of life we are less concerned with mastery of independent dance steps and more with just being part of the general dance. Such people have no need to stand out, make defining moves, or be better than others. Life is more participatory than assertive, and there is less need for self-assertion and self-definition. In the second half of life people live in the presence of God. In that reality, the brightness comes from within, a reflection of the divine that is more than adequate.

Those who live in the presence of God no longer have to prove that their ethnicity is superior, their group the best, their religion the only one that God approves, or that their place in society deserves special treatment. They become less preoccupied with amassing goods and services and focus instead on giving back to others a portion of what they have received. Their concern is no longer to have what they love, but rather to love what they have. When we meet such a shining person, we know that he or she is surely the goal of humanity and the delight of God.

Entry 5: The Second Journey, Part II

The second half of life journey is likened to the postcritical phase of life or a second simplicity. Paul Ricoeur speaks of it as a second naiveté or a second childhood. Whatever we call it, I believe this condition is the very goal of mature adulthood and mature religion. However, some people seem to miss the joy and clarity of the first simplicity, perhaps avoiding the interim complexity, and finally losing the great freedom and magnanimity of the second simplicity as well. We need to hold together all of the stages of life, and for some reason it all becomes quite "simple" as we approach our later years.

To embrace second half of life spirituality, we must first experience a full and healthy first half of life spirituality, for the two are related and progress in that order. The transition is not clear and practically undefinable, although generally speaking, elements of the second journey are present in the first journey, and elements of the first journey continue in the second. Ultimately, it is love and not knowledge that enables us to reach God in this life.

As previously noted, the transformation that brings us to the second half of life is often more about unlearning than learning. Perhaps it is simply a more profound learning. Life is more spacious now, the boundaries of the container having been enlarged by transformative experiences and relationships. For many people, the second half of life is characterized by seven transformational qualities:

1. Less fear and therefore less hostility. Because we have less need to eliminate the negative or fearful from our lives, there is less need to punish other people. Superiority complexes are shown to be useless, ego based, counterproductive, and often entirely wrong.

2. Less combativeness. By the second half of life we learn that most frontal attacks simply add to the amount of evil within. Along with an inflated self-image, they incite retaliation from those we attack.

3. Less need of attention. When "elders" speak, they need few words to make their point. Second simplicity has its own kind of brightness and clarity, but much of it is expressed nonverbally, and only when needed. In the first half of life, we are defined through differentiation; now we look for commonality. We do not need to dwell on the differences between people or exaggerate the problems. Creating dramas is boring.

4. Less assertion. In the second half of life it is good just to be a part of the general dance. We do not have to stand out or be better than others; life is more participatory than assertive, and there is no need for strong or further self-definition.

5. Less self-concern. At this stage we no longer have to prove we are the best, that our ethnicity is superior, our religion the only one accepted by God, or that our role and place in society deserve special treatment.

6. Less dogmatism. At this stage we are less condemning. We no longer see God as small, punitive, or tribal. Having defended signposts, now we arrive where the signs point. Our growing sense of spaciousness is no longer found mostly "out there" but especially "in here." The inner and the outer become one. In the second journey, we have less final opinions about things and people as we allow them to delight or sadden us. We no longer need to change or adjust other people in order to be happy ourselves. Ironically, we are more than ever before in a position to change others—but we do not need to—and that makes all the difference. Now we aid and influence others simply by being who we are.

7. Less possessiveness. At this stage we are no longer preoccupied with accumulating additional goods and services; rather, our desire and effort are to pay back to the world some of what we have received. Our concern is not so much to have what we love, but to love what we have—here and now. This is such a monumental change from the first half of life that it is almost the litmus test of whether we are in the second half of life at all.

Such transformation requires six steps: (1) forgiveness (repudiating retaliation or "getting even"); (2) prayer (learning to listen in silence); (3) changing one's attitude ("unlearning"); (4) quiet persuasion (becoming an elder statesman); (5) becoming an agent of change (which starts with actively working for peace); and (6) influencing events (indirectly rather than directly, by modeling the transformative qualities of the second simplicity).

If unlearning is a way to deeper spirituality, the following pathways represent "paradigm shifts," attitudinal transformations, in the journey from the first to the second half of life:

- Impatient to patient

- Fault-finding to greater acceptance

- Pessimistic to optimistic

- Stoical to joyful

- Independent to dependent

- Aloof to affectionate

- Self-centered to other-oriented

- Frugal to generous

Again, these observations do not represent precepts to be followed or new commandments to be obeyed. The second half of life is not about precepts or commandments, for there is only one guideline for the second half of life: to love the Lord your God with your entire mind, heart, soul, and strength, and your neighbor as yourself. The rest is commentary.

The great difference between transformed and nontransformed people is that transformed people live to serve, not to be served. Whole people see and create wholeness wherever they go.

Spirituality is like breathing—breathing deeply. When you breathe in, you are experiencing or replicating first half of life spirituality. When you breathe out, you are experiencing or replicating second half of life spirituality. To further clarify, I invite you to take three deep breaths, focusing on four elements of the breathing process. First, breathe in fully and hold your inhalation for a while, as long as comfortable. Then exhale and hold the exhalation for as long as comfortable. Do this three times at your own pace, paying attention to each nuance of your breath as you inhale, hold, exhale, and hold. Focus particularly on the empty space at the end of your exhalation.

In this moment, you have nothing to do, nothing to accomplish. For a time, you are giving yourself the gift of being fully present, fully alive, and fully expectant. Rest right here, fully in the moment, ready to receive, then ready to give. Welcome to second half of life spirituality! Receive it, embrace it, and rest fully in its risky fragility. This is the meaning of faith. If inhalation represents belief—walking by sight, clarity, affirmation, and certainty—exhalation represents faith—ambiguity, uncertainty, and unknowing. This is second half of life knowing and living, second half of life spirituality.

The Spiritual Journey, Part II

Entry 1: Three or More Halves of Life

WE SPEAK OF TWO halves of life, but in reality there are at least three, if we add the interim period called "midlife," and likely more. James Hollis, a Jungian analyst, notes that beyond the many subphases of life, there are four larger phases, each with a power to define the person's identity.[1] The first identity, *childhood*, is characterized by dependency of the ego on the world of the parents. The second identity begins at puberty. During *adolescence*, the emerging ego is malleable and prey to the influence of peers and pop culture. This phase has as its primary task the solidification of the ego, whereby a youth gains sufficient strength to leave parents, go into the larger world, and struggle for survival and the achievement of desire. Hollis calls the period from roughly twelve to forty the first adulthood. This identity, which may extend throughout one's life, is a provisional existence, lacking the depth and uniqueness that makes a person truly an individual.

The third phase of identity, the *second adulthood*, is launched when one's projections dissolve. In this crisis, one has the opportunity to become an individual, beyond the determinism of parents and cultural conditioning. Tragically, the repressive power of the psyche, with its reliance on authority, often keeps a person in thrall to cultural and parental complexes and thereby freezes development. Second adulthood is only attainable when the provisional identities have been discarded and the false self has died. The pain of such loss may be compensated by the rewards of the new life that follows, but the person in the midst of the midlife crisis may only experience the dying. The fourth identity, *mortality*, involves learning to live with the mystery of death and accepting its reality.

---

1. Hollis, *Middle Passage*, 23–27.

Another way to look at these shifting identities is to classify their different axes. In the first identity, childhood, the operative axis is the parent-child relationship. In the first adulthood the axis lies between ego and world. The ego struggles to project itself into the world and create a world within the world. In the second adulthood, both during and after midlife, the axis connects ego and Self. It is natural for consciousness to assume that it knows all and is running the show. When its hegemony is overthrown, the humbled ego then begins the dialogue with the Self, defined as the mystery within, concerned with the purposiveness of the organism. The fourth axis is Self-God or Self-Cosmos. This axis is framed by the cosmic mystery that transcends the mystery of individual existence. Without some relationship to the cosmos, we are constrained to lives of transience, superficiality, and aridity. Since the dominant culture offers little mythic mediation for the placement of self in a larger context, it is all the more imperative that the individual enlarge his or her vision.

Entry 2: Stages of Human Development, Part I

Most humans, ancient and modern alike, pattern their lives after some model, whether consciously or unconsciously. These models can be biological, social, psychological, cognitive, moral, ecological, religious, existential, or mystical. Healthy individuals are said to go through discernible stages of growth throughout their lifetime.

According to psychologist Erik Erikson (1902–1994), psychosocial development proceeds by critical steps, described as infancy (birth to 18 months), early childhood (2 to 3 years of age), preschool (3 to 5 years), school age (6 to 11 years), adolescence (12 to 18 years), young adulthood (19 to 40 years), middle adulthood (40 to 65 years), and maturity (65 to death). Each stage is marked by crisis, connoting not a catastrophe but a turning point, a crucial period of increased vulnerability and heightened potential. At such points achievements are won or failures occur, leaving the future to some degree better or worse but in any case, restructured. For each stage Erikson defined a basic conflict, important events, and outcomes.

The strength acquired at one stage is tested by the necessity to transcend it, meaning that the individual is able to take chances in the next stage with what was most vulnerably precious in the previous one. For example, healthy children will not fear life if their elders have integrity enough not to fear death.

A second developmental model is that of Lawrence Kohlberg (1927–1987), an American psychologist best known for his theory of stages of moral development. He delineates six stages of development, from pre-conventional to post-conventional morality as follows:

Pre-Conventional Morality

Stage 1: Obedience or Punishment Orientation

This is the stage that all young children start at (and a few adults remain in). Rules are seen as being fixed and absolute. Obeying the rules is important because it means avoiding punishment

Stage 2: Self-Interest Orientation

As children grow older, they begin to see that other people have their own goal and preferences and that often there is room for negotiation. Decisions are made based on the principle of "What's in it for me?" For example, an older child might reason: "If I do what mom or dad wants me to do, they will reward me. Therefore I will do it."

Conventional Morality

Stage 3: Social Conformity Orientation

By adolescence, most individuals have developed to this stage. There is a sense of what "good boys" and "nice girls" do and the emphasis is on living up to social expectations and norms because of how they impact day-to-day relationships.

Stage 4: Law and Order Orientation

By the time individuals reach adulthood, they usually consider society as a whole when making judgments. The focus is on maintaining law and order by following the rules, doing one's duty and respecting authority.

Post-Conventional Morality

STAGE 5: SOCIAL CONTRACT ORIENTATION

At this stage, people understand that there are differing opinions out there on what is right and wrong and that laws are really just a social contract based on majority decision and inevitable compromise. People at this stage sometimes disobey rules if they find them to be inconsistent with their personal values and will also argue for certain laws to be changed if they are no longer "working." Our modern democracies are based on the reasoning of Stage 5.

STAGE 6: UNIVERSAL ETHICS ORIENTATION

Few people operate at this stage all the time. It is based on abstract reasoning and the ability to put oneself in other people's shoes. At this stage, people have a principled conscience and will follow universal ethical principles regardless of what the official laws and rules are.

Entry 3: Stages of Human Development, Part II

In his book *Nature and the Human Soul* (2008), depth psychologist Bill Plotkin takes the four stages of human development—(a) childhood, (b) adolescence, (c) adulthood, and (d) elderhood—and develops an eight-stage model of human development called the Wheel of Life, an eightfold pathway from egocentricism to soulcentrism, a nature-based model that fully honors the deeply imaginative potentials of the human psyche. A wilderness guide and self-styled "agent of cultural evolution," Plotkin uses his model to show how healthy and holistic lifestyles should be rooted in a childhood of innocence and wonder, sprout into an adolescence of creative fire and mystery-probing adventures, blossom into an authentic adulthood of cultural artistry and visionary leadership, and finally ripen into an elderhood of wisdom and grace, tending both the social and natural world. His premise is that true adulthood is rooted in mystical affiliation with nature, experienced as a sacred calling, embodied in soul-infused work and mature responsibilities. This mystical affiliation is the very core of maturity, and it is precisely what Plotkin believes has been overlooked or even suppressed by mainstream Western society.

According to Plotkin, the eight stages, together with the passage from one stage to the next, are not defined by chronological age or social status but by the progress made with the developmental tasks encountered at each stage. Each transition involves loss and pain and entails a crisis for the conscious self. The stage of adolescence—beyond which most adults never move—holds the key to both individual development and human evolution. In this stage individuals develop their distinctive ego-based consciousness, which represents both their greatest liability as well as their greatest potential. If they are to become fully human and move to the stages of genuine adulthood, people in the adolescent stage must undergo an initiation process that requires letting go of the familiar and comfortable while submitting to a journey of descent into "the mysteries of nature and the human soul." Individuals who remain within the constraints of a largely adolescent world regress into "pathological adolescence," characterized by materialism, sexism, competitive violence, racism, egoism, and self-destructive patterns. Patho-adolescent societies are perpetuated by leaders and celebrities described as self-serving politicians, moralizing religious leaders, drug-induced entertainment icons, and greedy captains of industry. If society is going to develop soulcentrically, it must be overseen by councils of wise elders, not by assemblies of adolescent politicians and corporate officers.

Plotkin's stages, while correlating ideally with chronological, biological, and evolutionary age, are not primarily based on such phenomena, since people can remain locked in any of these stages, unable to progress further until they successfully complete the task(s) of that stage. According to Plotkin, one cannot skip a stage only to return later in hopes of moving on.

Committed to promoting a global ecological citizenry, the Wheel of Life provides a model for the human life cycle based on eight acts, offering a map for reaching the destination of becoming fully human. The Wheel, ecocentric in that it models individual human development from the perspective of nature's cycles, rhythms, and patterns, is also soulcentric in that it envisions the principal goal of maturation to be the conscious discovery and embodiment of soul. Understanding the human soul as being the very core of human nature, the eight developmental stages—early childhood, middle childhood, early adolescence, late adolescence, early adulthood, late adulthood, early elderhood, late elderhood—together constitute a single story, the story of a deeply fulfilling but nevertheless entirely human life.

Entry 4: Fowler's Stages of Faith

As humans grow by progressing physically, psychologically, emotionally, and even intellectually, so they undergo various stages of growth in their faith. Out of one's individuality flows a spirituality that also yearns for growth and expression. What Erikson contributed to our understanding of the stages of psychosocial development and Lawrence Kohlberg to the stages of moral development, so James Fowler (1940–2015) did for spirituality in developing seven stages of faith, from stage zero, called "primal faith," when infants and toddlers develop (or fail to develop) a sense of safety about the universe and the divine, to a sixth stage called "universalizing faith," a rarely reached stage of those who live their lives to the full in service of others without any real fears or worries. Most people plateau at what Fowler calls the "synthetic-conventional" stage, one arising in adolescence. At this stage authority is usually placed in individuals or groups that represent one's beliefs.

Fowler's stages of faith are described as

Stage 0: Primal Faith (0 to 2 years): This stage is characterized by early learning the safety of the environment. Under consistent nurture, children develop a sense of safety about the universe and the divine. Negative experiences (neglect and abuse) lead to distrust of the universe and the divine.

Stage 1: Intuitive-Projective (3 to 7 years): This is the stage of preschool children in which fantasy and reality often are mixed together. However, during this stage, our most basic ideas about God are usually learned from our parents and/or society.

Stage 2: Mythic-Literal (mostly in school children): When children become school-age, they start understanding the world in more logical ways. They generally accept the stories told to them by their faith community but tend to understand them in very literal ways. [Some people remain in this stage through adulthood.]

Stage 3: Synthetic-Conventional (arising in adolescence; ages 12 to adulthood): Most people move on to this stage as teenagers. At this point, their lives have grown to include several different social circles, which they need to pull together. When this happens, a person usually adopts some sort of all-encompassing belief system. However, at this stage, people tend to have a hard time seeing outside their box, not recognizing that they are "inside" a belief system. At this stage, authority is usually placed in individuals or groups that represent one's beliefs. [A great many adults remain in this stage.]

Stage 4: Individuative-Reflective (usually mid-twenties to late thirties): This is the tough stage, often begun in young adulthood, when people start seeing outside the box and realizing that there are other "boxes." They begin to examine their beliefs critically on their own and often become disillusioned with their former faith. Ironically, the Stage 3 people usually think that Stage 4 people have become "backsliders" when in reality they have actually moved forward.

Stage 5: Conjunctive Faith (mid-life crisis): It is rare for people to reach this stage before mid-life. This is the point when people begin to realize the limits of logic and start to accept life's paradoxes. As they begin to see life as a mystery, they often return to sacred stories and symbols but this time without remaining in a theological box.

Stage 6: Universalizing Faith (enlightened stage): Few people reach this stage; those who do, live their lives to the full in service of others without real worry or spiritual doubt.

In his book, *A Different Drum*, M. Scott Peck provides the following simplified version of Fowler's stages:

1. *Chaotic-Antisocial*—People in this stage are usually self-centered and often find themselves in trouble due to unprincipled living. If they do finally embrace the next stage, it often occurs in a very dramatic way.

2. *Formal-Institutional*—At this stage people rely on some sort of institution (such as a church) to give them stability. They become attached to the forms of their religion and become extremely upset when these are called into question.

3. *Skeptic-Individual*—Those who break with the previous stage usually do so when they start seriously questioning previously held values and beliefs. Frequently they end up non-religious and some stay here permanently.

4. *Mystical-Communal*—People who reach this stage start to realize that there is truth to be found in the previous two stages and that life can be paradoxical and mysterious. Those who reach this stage emphasize communal rather than individual concerns.

Entry 5: The Three Transformations of the Spirit

According to a parable attributed to the German philosopher Friedrich Nietzsche (1844–1900), human beings undergo three transformations of the spirit. The first is that of the camel, symbolic of childhood and youth. The camel gets down on its knees and says, "Put a load on me." The load represents the rules and regulations of upbringing. This is the time for obedience, receiving instruction and the information society requires of its citizens if they are to live a responsible life.

But when the camel is well loaded, it struggles to its feet and heads into the desert, where it is transformed into a lion—the heavier the load that has been carried, the stronger the lion will be. The task of the lion is to kill a dragon, and the name of the dragon is "Thou shalt." On every scale of this beast, a "thou shalt" is imprinted: some from time immemorial, others from that morning's headlines. Whereas the camel (the child) had to submit to the "thou shalts" and "thou shalt nots," the lion (the young adult) is to throw them off and come to his or her own realization.

When the dragon is thoroughly dead, with all its "thou shalts" overcome, the lion is transformed into a child moving out of its own nature, like a wheel impelled from its own hub. No more rules to obey; no more rules derived from the historical needs and tasks of the local society, but the pure impulse to living a life in flower.

How does a person know when it is time to move from first to second half of life spirituality, from dependence on religion to independence, from belief to faith? In the past, people went through rituals of passage, which allowed them to know when the were ready for flight. Today this is not always clear. But when it is time, your heart will tell you.

Young birds know when they are ready to fly. They stay in their nest or on their branch until they are ready to fly. When they follow their instinct, they are not mistaken. Likewise in art studios, there comes a moment when pupils have learned what the artist can teach them. Good teachers, like competent parents, prepare pupils for flight. Gifted students take risks, for they know when it is time to move on. What is true in nature, in the classroom, and at home is also true in the realm of the spirit. Once we have assimilated the craft of religion, its rules, beliefs, and rituals, we are ready for spiritual flight, following our heart but kept aloft by the updraft of God's Spirit. Like becoming adept at any skill, there will be a time of testing, with setbacks and failures. But the journey moves forward and is altogether exhilarating because we are fulfilling our purpose; for this we are made!

In his public lecture "The Seven Spiritual Laws of Success," the prominent Indian-American physician and philosopher Deepak Chopra notes that humans are goal-seeking organisms. Because worthy goals involve the ability to love and be compassionate, harmful addictive behavior qualifies as unworthy. From this perspective, a requisite quality for goal-seeking is the ability to hear one's inner voice, to be in touch with the Spirit within, one's true self and creative center. Living out of one's core, one's innermost being, Chopra believes, is what humans mean by "spirituality." Spirituality, simply defined, is "Self-awareness." You will notice I capitalize the word "Self," for this is both intentional and essential to a proper understanding of the concept.

Because it is easy to fall into a simplistic or merely humanistic view of spirituality, let me clarify what I mean. When I think of spirituality, I have in mind the account of Jesus healing a victim of blindness in Mark's gospel. According to Mark 8:22–26, when Jesus heals a blind man in the town of Bethsaida, the healing occurs in three stages. First, the man is blind. Next, Jesus lays hands on him, using saliva to anoint the man's eyes. However, the man's vision is blurry and indistinct. Lastly, Jesus again lays hands upon the blind man's eyes, whereupon his sight is fully restored, enabling him to see everything clearly.

The same pattern can be applied to spirituality (its three stages also understood as three distinct types of spirituality):

1. *self-consciousness.* This stage of awareness—the first half of life phase—denotes "self-awareness," a selfish, self-centered, egocentric state. Characterized by allegiance to the ego or false self, this stage represents deception and spiritual idolatry. In this stage, a false and dream-like state, humans are in the dark, unaware, and self-deceived.

2. *God-consciousness.* This phase, a transitional phase, is still idolatry, or, more accurately, monolatry, for as commonly understood, it represents institutional allegiance, attachment to ethical and man-made religious belief systems. This phase of spirituality, evident historically in salvation by effort approaches, can be likened to sleepwalking. In this stage participants are striving to make progress, but they are still in the dark. They are serving external requirements, pleasing an authoritarian deity.

3. *Self-consciousness.* This stage of awareness—the second half of life phase—is entered through realization, by awakening. Those thus

connected to their soul or core being are now "in the light," connected finally to their higher power, to pure consciousness. Such awareness—such living and thinking—is a gift of grace. This state of awareness cannot be earned, but, like the biblical pearl of great price, it can be found through diligent search and desire.

These stages represent the journey from darkness to light, illustrated in nature by the three phases of the twenty-four-hour day: night, twilight/dawn, and day.

The Five Halves of Life, Part I

Entry 1: Hindu Models for Life

WHEN SPEAKING OF LIFE'S journey, or more specifically, of a person's faith journey (including its religious and spiritual phases), it is beneficial to be guided by models, for all such journeys take place in particular contexts. All branches of religion/spiritual traditions around the world provide models for growth and progress within their tradition, including psychological, moral, and theological guidelines for sustained momentum.

Ancient Hindu society, for example, established a fourfold pattern for life, two stages for the social journey (student and householder phases), and two associated with the spiritual journey (retirement and homeless phases). The student phase begins after the rite of initiation, between the ages of eight and twelve, and lasts for twelve years. In this formative stage, proper behavior is cultivated and character is formed. The householder phase, viewed as the cornerstone of society, focuses on family, vocation, and community. During the retirement phase, individuals can withdraw from social obligation to discover the meaning of life and prepare for their rebirth after death. The *sannyasin* stage, open to members of the upper classes at any time, consists of an ascetic and homeless lifestyle, designed to eliminate individuality in hope of experiencing unity with eternal reality, thereby ending the recurring pattern of transmigration.

As a corollary to this developmental model, Hindus also devised four spiritual paths, *yogas*, or means of salvation:

- *karma yoga* (a spirituality of works intended for persons of active bent)

- *bhakti yoga* (a spirituality of devotion intended for persons of emotional bend)

- *jnana yoga* (a spirituality of knowledge intended for persons of reflective bent), and

- *raja yoga* (a spirituality of liberation or self-actualization for persons who are scientifically or experimentally inclined).

Unlike Hindu spirituality, which developed four parallel spiritualities or paths of salvation, it is important to note the holistic approach Jesus used in addressing questions about how best to fulfill God's will. Viewing love as the fulfillment of the Great Commandment, Jesus emphasized that his followers love God and neighbor not conditionally or out of obligation but passionately and wholeheartedly, with all their heart, soul, mind, and strength (Mark 12:30), uniting the four Hindu paths of salvation into one commitment.

Entry 2: Kierkegaard's Model for Life, Part I

In the Christian tradition, the noted Danish philosopher Søren Kierkegaard (1813–1855), made an important contribution to the life of faith in his formulation of three levels of existence or stages through which humans go in their ascent toward God. On the first level, which he labeled the *aesthetic stage*, individuals are ruled by their senses, in which case they can be called "sensual aesthetes." Such persons live solely for the present, and particularly for self-gratification. Aesthetes, characterized by the absence of either moral standards or religious faith, remain detached and uncommitted. Kierkegaard extended this attitude to include "the intellectual aesthete," the contemplative person who tries to stand outside of life and behold it as a spectator.

The aesthetic life, however, is not ultimately fulfilling, for it ends in boredom and despair. Aesthetes, recognizing that they are living inauthentically, find no remedy on this level. They must either remain there in boredom and despair or make a transition to the next level by an act of choice. Willing, not thinking, is the key. The act of choosing does not resolve the tension, for one must *either* remain at the first level *or* choose to move on. The antithesis remains.

The second level, called *the ethical stage*, requires that one abandon attitudes of selfishness and make commitments to others. Here moral standards and obligations are adopted, as dictated by reason. Cold detachment is left behind, for in this stage one embraces universal standards. The example Kierkegaard chose as the transition from aesthetic to moral consciousness is marriage, in which a person renounces the satisfaction of the sexual impulse according to passing attraction and enters the state of marriage, accepting all its obligations. This stage is meaningful and superior to the aesthetic level because it provides continuity and stability to life.

Entry 3: Kierkegaard's Model for Life, Part II

Whereas Kierkegaard believed sincerely in universal moral obligations, the ethical stage is not the end or goal of existence. The problem with this stage is that the ethical person remains committed to autonomy and self-sufficiency. The ethical hero recognizes self-sufficiency as sin, but believes he can overcome it by sheer willpower and ability. Eventually the ethical person comes to the awareness of inability to fulfill the moral law and becomes conscious of guilt and estrangement from God. The ethical person is once more confronted with a choice: either to continue in one's effort to fulfill the moral law, or move to a higher stage, to a life of faith. This requires an act of commitment, which Kierkegaard called a "leap of faith." In his own life Kierkegaard had found that the previous stages were based upon the "illusion of humanism," resulting in failure to recognize need for God. The third and final stage, which he called *the religious stage*, entails a life of faith. This is final because it recognizes the existence of God and the need to relate oneself wholly to God.

In each previous stage, Kierkegaard selected a figure from literature or history as an example. For the aesthetic stage he chose Don Juan, the classic figure from Spanish drama who lived solely for sensual pleasure and was unable to commit to a meaningful relationship with others. The ethical stage is typified by Socrates, who took his own life rather than compromise his moral standards. The example he selected for the religious stage was Abraham, whose trust of God and unwavering obedience led him to choose to sacrifice his only son Isaac, even in the face of absurdity, for to question God would be to place reason over faith.

Is such behavior justifiable or is it unethical? In selecting this example, Kierkegaard was not denying the validity of ethics. He stated that the individual who is called to break with the ethical must first be ethical, that is, must first have subordinated to universal morality. The break, when one is called to make it, is made in "fear and trembling" and not arrogantly or proudly. In this final stage, the ethical is not abolished but dethroned by a higher purpose or end, a phenomenon he described as the "teleological suspension of the ethical." The key to this final stage is not the commendable humanistic goal of universal duty to others, but the unqualified giving of oneself to God. If one doesn't go beyond the ethical, beyond moral obligation, one cannot properly say that one is related to God, or obedient to God. Ethical duty, he believed, must ultimately lead to God, but since it usually leads to humanity (i.e. to humanism), then this stage must be transcended. An absolute relationship to an absolute (God) requires a relative relationship to relative ends. For Kierkegaard, everything other than God is relative.

Entry 4: The Five Halves of Life Model, Overview and Phase 0

Understanding the term "half" symbolically rather than literally, it is possible to speak of five such dimensions or mindsets that people may acquire through life, including a preparatory stage or "half" (phase 0) and then two essentially secular/religious halves, which I call first and second half living and thinking (phases 1A and 1B), themselves mirroring two spiritual phases called first and second half of life spirituality (phases 2A and 2B), configured as follows:

1. Preparatory Half (phase 0): preconventional morality (childhood and adolescence)

2. First Half Living and Thinking (phase 1A): conventional morality (late adolescence through adulthood)

3. Second Half Living and Thinking (phase 1B): postconventional morality (late adolescence through adulthood)

4. First Half of Life Spirituality (phase 2A): conventional religiosity (late adolescence through adulthood)

5. Second Half of Life Spirituality (phase 2B): postconventional spirituality (late adolescence through adulthood).

In this model, phase 0 corresponds to the Hindu pre-initiation stage, to Kohlberg's stages 1 and 2, to Fowler's stages 0, 1, and 2, as well as to Kierkegaard's sensual or aesthetic stage, in that at this stage of life, individuals are ruled by the senses, concerned primarily with self-gratification, and live for the present. Individuals in phase 0 (including most children, youth, adolescents, and some adults) may have special and unique spiritual dispositions and experiences, but such experience is immature and unformed. On the whole, their beliefs, behavior, and outlook is best characterized as preparatory or preconventional, since their character and personality, like their morality and brains, is mostly borrowed, imitated, untested, and not yet fully formed. This phase revolves around the mental function of sorting nearly everything into one of two categories (things are either permitted or prohibited, others are either friend or foe, and one is either happy or sad). For that reason, in stage 0, you set out to master the mental skills of dualism, of seeing the world in twos (this or that, in or out, right or wrong). Stage 0 is the baseline of what being raised means in our culture. Here one is taught the difference between right and wrong and other basic dualisms.

Entry 5: The Five Halves of Life Model, Phase 1A

At some point in their socializing growth, youth begin accommodating to those around them, joining peer groups and aspiring to be admired and respected by others. Entering the first half of living and thinking, such individuals are shaping, developing, and testing their identity. Authorities—parents, grandparents, teachers, political and religious leaders—are central to this phase. Phase 1A is the phase of authority as well as of dualism. This phase corresponds to the Hindu student stage, to Kohlberg's stages 3 and 4, to Fowler's stage 5, and to initial aspects of Kierkegaard's ethical stage. While some individuals at this point become relatively autonomous, the majority desire to be like their elders, valuing and depending on their authority. They trust authorities and wish to please them, and they aspire to be as certain and all-knowing as they are. As far as they are concerned, the authorities know everything, and they do not, so they feel highly dependent on them. Before long, they find out that the authorities in their life dislike or distrust other authorities, and their dualism adds a new category: us versus them. This social dualism creates a strong sense of loyalty and identity among "us." It also creates a strong sense of anxiety and even hostility about "them," the "others," the "outsiders," and the "outcasts." Phase 1A is built on trust, because at that stage, trust is an absolute necessity, a matter of survival. Simple trust and unquestioning loyalty are what matters in phase 1A.

While this phase works well with adolescents and young adults, many people spend their entire lives in phase 1A, submitting to authorities and following all the rules. Then, when it is time for them to become authorities themselves, they demand the same submission from the next generation that they themselves gave to the previous generation. For that reason, it shouldn't be a surprise that faith and religion are a strictly phase 1A phenomenon for millions, even billions, of people.

Topic 6

The Five Halves of Life, Part II

Entry 1: The Five Halves of Life Model, Phase 1B

THUS FAR, PHASE 1A may feel like a school to help people learn the basic morals necessary for independence. However, at some point, this phase becomes confining or restrictive, and individuals begin to question whether authorities are always right. They may even question whether rules are always absolute and appropriate. This may happen at twelve or twenty-two or forty-five, but eventually, many enter phase 1B. If phase 1A is about dualism and dependence, phase 1B is about pragmatism and independence. People in this phase recognize they have their own lives to live, and they have to find a way to become who they are on their own.

In phase 1A they were drawn to authority figures who told them what to think and do, but in phase 1B they seek out coaches who teach them how to think for themselves and help them develop their own goals, along with their own skills to attain those goals. In phase 1A they saw life as a matter of survival, but in phase 1B they see life as a game, as a contest of competing and winning. In phase 1A everything was either known or knowable, but in phase 1B, everything is learnable and doable, if only they can find the right models, mentors, and coaches, and master the right techniques, skills, and know-how. Phase 1B corresponds to the Hindu householder stage, to Kohlberg's stage 5, and to aspects of Kierkegaard's ethical and religious stages.

When people run into problems with phase 1A living and thinking, some may temporarily or permanently resort to stage 0 behavior and belief, living solely for pleasure and ego-gratification. However, many phase 1A individuals abandon dualism and pragmatism, together with authoritarian leaders, dogmatic mindsets, and moralistic standards, and commit instead to global and pluralistic values, loving others selflessly, simplifying lifestyle, living generously and compassionately, committing to social, ecological, political, and economic issues and concerns. Becoming atheists, agnostics, or merely nonbelievers, such individuals embody Fowler's stage 6, only achieving this stage secularly and nonspiritually.

While we are now familiar with the expression "the first and second halves of life," we should not, indeed we cannot equate them with first and second half of life spirituality. While there are similarities and overlap between these formulations, the first expression refers essentially to chronology, distinguishing immaturity from maturity, youth and adulthood from midage and old age, starting life from concluding life.

By contrast, first and second half of life spirituality, while often working in tandem with first and second half of life living and thinking, is a way of life and thought that though religious in nature, is centered on encounter with deity/divine Spirit, with opening to grace as the foundational event. However, for many if not for most individuals, piety, religion, morality, and even culture take the place of spirituality. In such cases, nominal religion becomes religiosity, a substitute for authentic spirituality, and in speaking of religiosity, we find we are no longer describing spirituality but rather an acculturated form of first half of life living and thinking. For many people, particularly those brought up in evangelical Christian homes, phase 1A (first half living and thinking) and phase 2A (first half of life spirituality) are experienced concurrently, for they find themselves living dualistically, adapting to secular and religious rules and guidelines simultaneously.

Entry 2: The Five Halves of Life Model, Phase 2A

According to the Five Halves of Life model, it is quite natural for many children brought up in traditional Christian households to bypass phases 1A and 1B altogether and enter phase 2A spirituality at an early age. As is true of phase 1A, phase 2A, understood as a moral/religious phase common to evangelical Christianity, this stage is centered on acquiring essential religious beliefs and mastering dualistic mental skills such as sorting things into opposing categories such as right or wrong, true or false, sacred or secular, good and evil, and others as friends or foes. Authorities such as parents, teachers, and religious leaders are central to this way of being religious or spiritual. Similar to phase 1A, phase 2A commonly corresponds to the Hindu student phase, to Kohlberg's stages 3 and 4, and to Fowler's stage 3. However, unlike phase 1A, phase 2A incorporates elements of Kierkegaard's ethical and religious stages, in that it combines morality with a life of faith.

In my experience and from my vantage point as a scholar of spirituality and religious studies, the entry point to authentic spirituality, unlike much moral and religious belief and behavior, is not ritual or indoctrination, although these can be catalysts for first half of life spirituality, but rather a personal or individual encounter with the divine. This experience, called a "second birth" by evangelicals, profession of faith and baptism by Baptists, speaking in tongues or Spirit-filled living by Pentecostals, confirmation by Catholics, or Bar Mitzvah by Jews, is frequently the foundational experience for first half of life spirituality. Such events are usually euphoric, but such euphoria is often short-lived, for this experience is frequently followed by conformity, rigid religious belief, and moralistic behavior.

Because phase 2A spirituality is highly dualistic, such dualism is divisive and, like phase 1A, it creates a strong sense of loyalty and identity. It also creates a strong sense of anxiety and even hostility toward "outsiders," "backsliders," and "outcasts." At some point in the faith journey, phase 2A believers are no longer content merely to listen to a sermon by an authority figure; they want to learn methods of studying the Bible for themselves. Learning and studying, thinking for themselves and reaching their own conclusions, are part of what it means to be a good phase 2A believer. Such people become active consumers in the religious market. Every year, they need more sermons, books, radio and TV shows, podcasts, conferences, courses, retreats, camps, churches, and mission trips. For some phase 2A people, their faith never exceeds the authoritarian, dualistic faith of phase 2A spirituality, while others never exceed the inquisitive, pragmatic side of dogmatic faith. Others, however, outgrow this phase altogether, questioning their religious goals, needs, and priorities.

When people run into problems with phase 2A spirituality, some transfer to another faith community. Other disillusioned phase 2A believers temporarily or permanently revert to phase 1 standards, perspectives, and forms of living. When phase 2A people find religious teaching or programming doesn't produce the results they expect, many sincere believers simply amp up their effort, assuming the fault is their own. Many modern individuals, however, experience a profound loss of religious confidence, and their phase 2A spirituality starts to collapse. For most such believers, there is no going back, at least not in the long term. Having felt increasingly alienated from phase 2A spiritual dualism and theological dogmatism, they lose faith in both authoritarian leaders and success coaches, whether inside or outside the church. Both types of leaders made promises they couldn't deliver, and neither type honestly faced life's deeper questions and challenges.

Entry 3: The Five Halves of Life Model, Phase 2B

While some phase 2A believers start doubting the whole faith project, others aren't so easily satisfied. Their quest for honesty and depth burns like a fire in the belly and they move into phase 2B spirituality. If such phase 2A believers remain open and patient, many encounter a moment of crisis, and they find themselves actors in a deeper narrative that embraces and integrates all things, producing a way to see things whole again. This second awakening produces seekers, transformed by what might be called "an experience of sacred mystery." Something has happened to them—a mystical experience, something traumatic, a relationship, a sudden realization, a wilderness experience, an experience of "something more"—and the word "God" became meaningful once again, only this time not as a reference to a supernatural being "out there" but to the sacred at the center of existence, the holy mystery that is all around us and within us. No longer a mere idea or an article of belief external to oneself, God has become an element of experience. Such persons have reached phase 2B spirituality (also called *second naiveté*), a state where they participate in religious rituals because they are meaningful and not because they are required, where they hear ancient biblical stories as "true" while knowing them as not literally true.

Looking back, they discover that they still retain powerful and valuable treasures gained in previous phases. Though nondualists, they appreciate the lessons of dualism, which taught them to distinguish right from wrong and good from evil, and to care about their choices. From earlier phases, they also learned to be curious and flexible. They also learned that different phases of life operate by different sets of rules. In addition to becoming independent, self-motivated, and self-managed adults who take responsibility for their own successes and failures, they also learned that doubt and perplexity bring some of the greatest spiritual gifts life has to offer, gifts such as humility, honesty, courage, and sensitivity. Critical of their own critical thinking, skeptical of their own skepticism, they begin to wonder, hope, and imagine, and they dare to believe that there is a better second half of life, a better half of spirituality. To maintain momentum, to keep growing and developing, however, requires a kind of dying, a death to ego or pride, a relinquishment of our right to judge, to know, and to control. You might call this a death to privilege, superiority, or supremacy, as seekers realize that all people share in the human condition.

Phase 2B spirituality builds on "the still more excellent way of love" described by Paul in his letter to the Corinthians (1 Cor 12:31–14:1). In this passage, Paul makes clear that nearly everything religious people strive for will eventually be embraced by something deeper. Even faith and hope don't have the last word. Only love, he says, is the more excellent way. In this phase, we can finally accept that all our knowing, past and present, is partial (1 Cor 13:12). Phase 2B seekers finally see authority figures as mortal and fallible human beings. This awareness also allows them to find their identity in new ways in relation to others; not in phase 2A dependence on fallible authority figures but in the more mature interdependence of nonduality. This humility before others morphs into the realization that no statement about God—or even about what is true—can be final or complete.

This new realization—likened to a second naiveté, a second simplicity or innocence best described as transcendence, combines the best of the conservative and the best of the progressive positions, because it brings along or includes the previous stages rather than leaving them behind. Phase 2B spirituality eventually matures into a higher spirituality, continuing in an ascending spiral of growth and discovery that lasts as long as life itself. Far from feeling they have finally arrived, phase 2B seekers finally begin to understand that arrival has never been the goal.

Corresponding to aspects of Hindu retirement and *sannyasin* stages as well as to Kohlberg's stage 6, Fowler's stage 6, and advanced existential aspects of Kierkegaard's religious stage, phase 2B spirituality allows seekers to discover amazing truths. For example, they discover that spirituality is about love; that knowing is loving; that they know ourselves by loving ourselves; that they know others by loving them; that they know God by loving ourselves and others. Those who reach phase 2B spirituality do not experience certainty, however, for that is the concern of those in earlier phases. Phase 2B seekers never feel they have arrived. They are not obsessed with misguided notions of certainty or supremacy—more the opposite. Committed to the faith journey, they know there is no such thing as certainty in faith. Faith, like all creativity, flourishes not in certainty but in questioning, not in security but in venturing. In phase 2B spirituality, it is trust that matters, and qualities such as peace, harmony, joy, relationships, intimacy, and unity.

Entry 4: The Five Halves of Life Model, Conclusion

While some form of awakening (spiritual conversion or "spiritual rebirth") may be foundational for second half of life spirituality, this experience differs from similar first half of life conversion in that for this second "half" of life, such an experience is not based on a decision one makes or a commitment one controls. Rather, this experience is an absolute gift of grace, for it comes more as a realization or revelation than as an act of the will. Unlike entrance into first half of life spirituality, this second experience is best described as a realization or awakening, for such transformation simply happens over time, more like a process than an event, and it may take time before individuals become conscious of the changes within themselves. More commonly, awareness occurs retrospectively, brought to our attention by those around us who notice the difference in our attitude, nature, and demeanor.

According to the five halves of life model, spirituality is not a specific way of living and thinking, nor a way of being moral or religious, but rather is a mature and selfless way of being. While first half of spirituality (phase 2A) may be initiated by individuals and can look like religious living and thinking, second half of spirituality (phase 2B) is initiated and led by the Divine Spirit. In both cases, individuals are oriented consciously and unconsciously toward the Divine, understood to be present both immanently and transcendently.

While individuals can describe their own experience of the second spiritual journey and even serve as mentors, they cannot define or outline the journey for others. This is due both to the uniqueness of the journey and to a subtle factor, known by generations of mystics and spiritual masters but elusive to many of our contemporaries: One does not choose this second spiritual journey; rather it chooses you. It finds you by means of your soul, your personal center and true home, the source of your true belonging. The soul comes to our aid through dreams, deep emotion, love, the quiet voice of guidance, synchronicities, revelations, hunches, and visions, and at times through illness, nightmares, and terrors. This is the identity that defines us, aligning us with our powers of nurturing, transforming, and creating, with our powers of presence and wonder. It is the soul that guides us, preparing the way and declaring us ready for this further journey.

As you may have guessed, the use of the phrase "five halves of life" in this chapter serves as a *koan*, that is, as an irrational riddle designed to stimulate your deepest intuition and to help you remain open to the limitless possibilities associated with spirituality. Viewed literalistically or on an elementary level, there can only be two halves of life, rather than three, four, or five. From this perspective, the five halves of life model is reducible to two halves or dimensions of life, one set of halves for the false self or ego and one set for the True Self or soul, both preceded by a preparatory or preliminary phase or dimension.[1]

Entry 5: Analogies from Physics and Music

While the notion of "five halves of life" remains speculative, we find analogies in the realms of physics and music. For example, physicists speak of four dimensions of reality: height, width, depth, and time. The first three aspects apply to all objects in space, whether stationary or in motion. Each aspect can be apprehended with the senses, particularly with sight. The fourth dimension, time, is intuitive and cannot be apprehended directly by the senses. Like the four dimensions of objects, there are four basic forces in nature—gravitational, electromagnetic, strong, and weak—that govern how particles interact and how certain particles decay. All known forces of nature can be traced to these fundamental forces. Physicists have long sought to show that these four basic forces are simply different manifestations of the same fundamental force. Such attempts led them to quantum physics and to explanations of a Grand Unified Theory found in particle physics and in frameworks such as string theory. In 2016, scientists investigating the forces that control the natural world posited the possibility of a fifth fundamental force, calling it X17. Working with decayed isotopes of beryllium and helium, they noticed abnormal or atypical behavior that led to the conclusion of an unknown force or particle responsible for the anomalous behavior, a completely new kind of fundamental boson yet unknown. Scientists are hoping that such a fundamental particle in nature could point to a fifth force connecting normal matter we see with dark matter we cannot see.

---

1. The distinction between False and True Self is discussed in topic 7 below.

Like the four dimensions of objects in space and time, researchers now speak of a fifth dimension, considered a micro-dimension rather than one of the four known dimensions. The fifth dimension emerged when physicists sought to connect all parts of the universe in a way that make sense, which could provide a framework that unifies disparate elements such as gravity, electromagnetism, and time with photons and light in a unifying fifth dimension.

In music theory we find the phenomenon known as the circle of fifths (obvious to anyone who has played scales on a musical instrument such as a piano). Simply put, the principle begins with the note of C and the key of C major (which has no sharps or flats), and then moves up in steps of perfect fifths through every key (beginning with one sharp and ending with one flat), until it returns to C major. In classical music from Western culture, a perfect fifth is the interval from the first to the last of five consecutive nots in a diatonic scale. The perfect fifth spans seven semitones (for example, the interval from C to G is a perfect fifth, as the note G lies seven semitones above C). Like physics and music, spirituality also searches for balance and unity, a symmetry achieved paradigmatically by the five halves of life model.

Death of the False Self and Resurrection of the True Self

Entry 1: The Two Selves

THE ULTIMATE ADVENTURE, THE grandest game, the greatest challenge, is the spiritual transformation of the self. As I discuss in my 2019 book, *Walking on Water*, the role of authentic spirituality is letting go of the false self, one's incomplete self trying to pass for one's True Self. Our True Self, our inherent soul, is that part of us that sees reality accurately, truthfully. It is divine breath passing through us, dwelling with us. Our false self is the egoic self that is limited and constantly changing. It masquerades as true and permanent but in reality is passing, tentative, and fearful of change. It is that part of us that will eventually die. The role of true spirituality, of mature religion, is to help speed up this process of dying to the false self.

Not surprisingly, we cannot accomplish—or even understand—what we have not been told to look for or to expect. This staggering change of perspective—that our ego is not our True Self—is what Jesus came to convey to humanity. It led Thomas Merton, the Trappist monk who first suggested use of the term false self, to his radical rediscovery of the meaning of Jesus' teaching that his followers must lose their false self in order to discover their True Self (see Mark 8:35).

This realization—what some people call "mindfulness" and mystics call "being present"—is the heart of religious transformation (meaning, "to change forms"). For Christians, the model and exemplar of such transformation is Jesus, who came to tell us—and show us—that our human form is also divine, that what is human also shares in the divine nature, a divinely implanted reality that can be experienced here and now, in our present mortal state. Initially, that possibility might sound far-fetched, but I assure you, that concept is both true and truly Christian.

The Greek word *theosis*, often used by Eastern Christians and perhaps best translated as "divinization" or "deification," speaks of this reality. Bishop Irenaeus taught the concept in the second century when he wrote that "God had become what we are, that He might bring us to be even what He is Himself."[1] Likewise, Bishop Athanasius of Alexandria at the end of the fourth century declared: "Jesus Christ was made human so that he might make us gods"[2] The clearest biblical antecedents for this teaching are 2 Peter 1:3–4, "His divine power has given us everything needed for life and godliness . . . so that through them you may escape the corruption that is in the world . . . and may *become participants in the divine nature*," and 2 Corinthians 5:16–17, "From now on, therefore, we regard no one from a human point of view. . . . So if anyone is in Christ, there is a new creation: everything old has passed away; see, everything has become new!" Elsewhere Paul uses words like "adopted" (Gal 4:5) and "joint heirs with Christ" (Rom 8:17) to make the same point.

Unfortunately, many people today, including religious and non-religious conservatives and other traditionalists, have become and remain quite rigid in their thinking, living, and believing because they have been taught that happiness, success, and stability require adherence to the religious status quo, and with it unquestioned obedience to the guardians of tradition. Such people are often moral and productive—even model citizens—but they simply never learned much about wisdom, paradox, or mystery, and their centrality to the faith traditions they espouse. When so many religious practitioners, including most professional clergy, attend worship and observe rituals faithfully without experiencing spiritual transformation at any deep level, religion becomes a duty that actually prevents transformation from taking place. This has been going on for centuries, and in all faith traditions.

In Jesus' day, most of his contemporaries, particularly social, religious, and political leaders, simply could not see what he saw (Matt 13:13–17). This was not due to Jesus' unique identity or access to truth, for he keeps saying, in effect, "You should all know better. You do not know your own wonderful Jewish tradition." The same could be said of conventional

1. *Against Heresies* 4, 38.
2. *De Incarnatione* 54, 3.

Muslims, Buddhists, Hindus, or Christians today, "You do not know your own wonderful religious heritage."

Like any true reformer or prophet, Jesus evaluates his tradition from within, by its own criteria and its own documents. This is what I hope to do here for Christianity or any religion. Too often, religion offers doctrinal conclusions, additional competing truth claims in the increasingly growing marketplace of religious claims, but seldom does it give people a vision or process whereby they can legitimate those truth claims for themselves by inner experience and actual practice. As German Jesuit theologian Karl Rahner often remarked, "Devout Christians of the future will either be 'mystics' or else cease being anything at all."[3]

Entry 2: Death of the False Self

Mature religion talks about the death of any notion of a separate, false self, while recognizing that only a deep security in a larger love will give you the courage to do that. The True Self can let go because it is secure at its core. Our false self, however, does not let go easily.

As Jesus and other great spiritual teachers made clear, there is a self that must be found and another that must be renounced. This teaching is found in each gospel (see Matt 10:39; 16:25; Mark 8:35; Luke 9:24), but is central to John's gospel, where it is coupled with "dying to the self": "unless a grain of wheat falls into the earth and dies, it remains just a single grain; but if it dies, it bears much fruit" (John 12:24). Hence, "those who love their life lose it [that is, their false self], and those who hate their life [their false self] in this world will keep it [their True Self] for eternal life" (John 12:25; see also 1 Cor 15:36–37, 42).

In one way or another, almost all religions say that you must die before you die—and then you will know what dying means, and what it does not mean. What it does mean, of course, is the relinquishment of selfish, possessive living, of egoic existence. The ego self is the self before death; some form of death—psychological, spiritual, relational, or physical—is the only way we will loosen our ties to our small and separate false self. Only then does it return in a new shape, which we call the soul, the True Self, or the Risen Christ.

There are four major splits from reality that we have all made in varying degrees to create our false self:

3. Cited in Rohr, *Naked Now*, 38.

- We split from our shadow self[4] and pretend to be our idealized self.

- We split our mind from our body and soul, and live in our minds.

- We split life from death and try to live without any "death."

- We split ourselves from other selves and try to live apart, superior, and separate.[5]

Each of these illusions must be overcome, either in this world or at the moment of physical death. Spirituality, pure and simple, is overcoming these splits from Reality. Anything less than the death of the false self is inadequate religion. The false self must die for the True Self to live, or, as Jesus put it, "If I do not go, the Advocate [the Holy Spirit] will not come to you" (John 16:7). Theologically speaking, what this verse is telling us is that Jesus (a good person) still had to die for the Christ (the universal presence) to arise. This is the pattern of transformation, where the letting go of the original indispensable self results in the arrival of a better reality.

Your True Self sees truthfully and will live forever. Your false self is constantly changing and will eventually die. Your false self is your necessary warm-up, the ego part of you that establishes your separate identity, especially in the first half of life. It is your incomplete self trying to pass for your whole self. The role of true spirituality, of mature religion, is to help speed up this process of dying to the false self. Whatever one calls it, true spirituality is the form of living embodied by Jesus and taught by the Buddha. Such calm, egoless approach to life is invariably characteristic of people at the highest levels of doing and loving in all cultures and religions. These are the ones we call sages or holy ones.

Without what Jesus called "the sign of Jonah" (see Matt 12:39–40)—the pattern of new life only through death—Christianity remains a largely impotent ideology, another way to "win" instead of the "way of the cross" characterized by Jonah, Jeremiah, Job, John the Baptist, and Jesus. Viewed this way, Jesus become the teacher of the path rather than the cosmic problem-solver. The Jonah-Job-Jesus pattern has been hard for Westerners to

---

4. The shadow self, something everyone possesses, represents the least developed part of one's personality. The shadow uses relatively childish and primitive forms of judgment and perception, often as an escape from the conscious personality and in defiance of conscious standards. One's shadow includes "good" qualities as well as "bad" or "shameful" qualities that one denies. As one makes room for one's polarities, one becomes healthier and more open to transforming grace.

5. Rohr, *Diamond*, 29.

recognize and accept, but it is taught by what we call Eastern religions. The sign of Jonah is at the heart of the matter.

Psychologically, the large fish represents "the power of life locked in the unconscious. Metaphorically, water is the unconscious, and this creature in the water is the life or energy of the unconscious, which has overwhelmed the conscious personality and must be disempowered, overcome, and controlled. . . . In the story of Jonah, the hero is swallowed and taken into the abyss to be later resurrected—a variant of the death-and-resurrection theme."[6]

The egoic self is real, precious, unique, but temporary, for your false self is what changes, passes, and ends when you die. There is no escape from death when the "you" is the egoic self. It is a manifestation of the True Self, but it tends to forget this and imagines itself to be apart from God rather than a part of God. However, such thinking is in error. There is no "you" separate from God, just as there is no wave separate from the ocean. When you die—psychologically and spiritually but also physically—you are still what you were and are: holy, sacred, and immortal.

Entry 3: Resurrection of the True Self

If all you have at the end of your life is your false self, there will not be much to eternalize. However, there is no death when the "you" is the divine Self, for the True Self lives forever. When you are connected to the Whole, you no longer need to defend or protect the isolated part. You are now connected to something Real, eternal. When you are able to move beyond your false self—at the right time and in the right way—it will feel like freedom and liberation, as if you had lost nothing.

It is no surprise that we humans would deny death's certain coming, fight it, and seek to avoid the demise of the only self we have known. This process of transformation is something we both deeply desire and desperately fear. It is the phenomenon Rudolph Otto termed the *mysterium tremendum*, an experience both alluring and frightful at the same time. Originally described in the language of symbol and myth, this experience has been acted out in ritual and other kinds of human activity long before it became a topic of philosophical and theological discussion. It is the union that will liberate us, yet we resist and flee.

6. Campbell, *Power of Myth*, 146.

The path of dying and rising is exactly what in-depth spiritual teaching must address. It is the letting go of all you think you are, moving into a world without any experienced context, and becoming the person you always were at depth and yet did not know on the surface. The surrender of our false self in the final days and hours in any conscious dying have been called "enlightenment at gunpoint" by Kathleen Dowling Singh, a woman who spent her life in hospice work.

We put off enlightenment by decades if we are not present at deaths—and births. Remember, salvation is not so much a matter of *if* as *when* you get it, and maybe how much we can handle.[7] It makes us wonder why we have turned the spiritual journey into a forced march or into a game of *Survivor*, instead of a joyous proclamation of this necessary but good process of surrender into love. The reason seems obvious; it is because the false self prefers win-lose over win-win, even, strangely enough, when it ends up defining itself as a loser. The ego will always choose trumped-up competition over calm cooperation. Such a mindset—more "hell" than "heaven," seems almost the American way.

Once you know you are sharing in "the force field of resurrection," you can always live within it, drawing from its power.[8] Nevertheless, the price of such momentous realization is that you must first go into the tomb with Jesus, "so that, just as Christ was raised from the dead by the glory of the Father, so we too might walk in newness of life" (Rom 6:4).

As the mystics and sages teach, the path of dying and rising is one continuous movement. It begins with learning to love one's life, and then with allowing oneself to die into it—and never to die away from it. Once death is joyfully incorporated into life, you are already in heaven, and there is no possibility or fear of hell. This is the Way, modeled by Jesus and enacted by his followers. "The Gospel is not a fire insurance policy for the next world, but a life assurance policy for this world."[9]

Entry 4: Learning How to See, Part I

As all mystics know and teach, spirituality is about seeing rightly, for "how one sees is what one sees." As Jesus says in Matthew 6:22, "The eye is the lamp of the body. So, if your eye is healthy, your whole body will be full

7. Rohr, *Diamond*, 141.

8. Rohr, *Diamond*, 144.

9. Rohr, *Eager to Love*, xxii.

of light." Moses could never have seen burning bushes as divine, could never have persevered with so much unknowing, unless he had moved to a higher level of seeing. William Blake, the seminal mystic poet who worked to bring about change both in the social order and in common ways of thinking, taught that "All we need to do is cleanse the doors of perception, and we shall see things as they are—infinite."

While Western religions have been preoccupied with telling people *what* to know and believe, mystics approach things differently, teaching people *how* to see. That, according to Luke's gospel, is what took place when the resurrected Jesus joined two ordinary travelers on their way home in Emmaus. He invites them to "open up" by telling their story of heartbreak. In the process, he explains to them his own life narrative. Through this act of intimacy and disclosure, they learn to see; their eyes are opened "and they recognized him" (Luke 24:31). Later that day, Jesus also appears to his sequestered disciples, transforming their vision from despondency to resurrection reality (Luke 24:36–49).

In the gospels, Jesus praises God for hiding divine wisdom "from the wise and the intelligent" and for having revealed it "to infants" (Matt 11:25). What is it that the learned and the clever often miss, and why is it that only infants and children see it? The learned and self-sufficient ones often see themselves as "having arrived," and by such arrogance, they remain outsiders to divine mystery. Their resistance and cleverness block its possibilities and hinder its reciprocity. Because of their vulnerability and dependence, children are avid learners, open to growth and newness. That is why children have a head start. When vulnerable exchange happens, there is always an augmentation of being on both sides. We are improved people afterward, bigger and better selves.

Entry 5: Learning How to See, Part II

During the medieval period, two influential Christian philosophers at the monastery of St Victor in Paris—Hugh of St. Victor and Richard of St. Victor—wrote that humanity was given three different sets of eyes. The first was the eye of sensation, the second the eye of reason, and the third the eye of understanding. The third eye—the mystical gaze—builds on the first two, yet goes further. It represents the full goal of all seeing and knowing.

The first two ways of seeing, when separated from the third, result in dualistic thinking, an "us versus them" way of seeing, the foundation of much violence and discontent in the world. The third way of seeing—typifying the seer, the poet, the saint, and the authentic mystic—grasps the whole picture. Today's world has many eccentrics, fanatics, rebels, and self-promotors. What the world needs is more mystics who see with all three sets of eyes. Such people are both humble and compassionate, for knowing that they do not know, they experience the unknowable.

Some call such knowing conversion, some call it enlightenment, some transformation, and some holiness. This way of knowing is Paul's "third heaven," where he "heard things that are not to be told, that no mortal is permitted to repeat" (2 Cor 12:2–4). Far too often, organized religion has a stake in keeping members in the first or second heaven, for this keeps them coming back, and keeps clergy in business. This is not always intentional, but rather an extension of the principle that you can lead others only as far as you yourself have gone. Lacking the contemplative gaze, such leaders remain functionaries and technicians, their parishioners without the resources to guide them into Mystery. Theological training without spiritual experience is protectionist, not progressive.

What I call the contemplative gaze is not a technique for acquiring benefit, for getting ahead, or even a requirement for entry into heaven; nor is it a pious exercise that somehow pleases God. It is much more like practicing heaven now.

Paradoxically, if we misuse spiritual awareness, or keep it to ourselves, it "hides," and we cannot go deeper. This is why many remain at the level of mere "religion," and it is surely what Jesus means when he says, "For to those who have, more will be given, and they will have an abundance; but for those who have nothing, even what they have will be taken away" (Matt 13:12). How does the "secret" of God's kingdom, of God's reality and nature, become "unhidden"? It is disclosed when people stop hiding—from God, themselves, and others. The emergence of our True Self discloses the secret of God's kingdom, the mystery of reality.

All who witness this mystery, who experience its reality, "become children of God" (John 1:12), and, as Paul puts it, if children, then also "heirs of God and joint heirs with Christ" (Rom 8:15–17; see also Gal 4:7). While the Judeo-Christian tradition tells us we are already children of God, made in "God's image and likeness" (Gen 1:26–27), most of us have no clue what this means, and far fewer live out of its resources.

Twenty-five hundred years ago the Indian sage Siddhartha Gautama—the historical Buddha—experienced enlightenment. After years of training in the austerities of his native Hinduism, he was no closer to Truth than before he began. Then something changed. He took responsibility for his own awakening. He ceased to walk the path his teachers followed and simply sat down. He sat beneath a large fig tree in Bodh Gaya, India, and observed what he could of the world within and without. Then the veil lifted, and he realized what he was unable to see previously. Transformed, he knew what he was—he was awake.

Dual and Nondual Consciousness

Entry 1: The Dualist Dilemma, Part I

Two necessary paths move us forward in life: a journey outward and a journey inward. To live adventurously means to take risks, to try new things, to embrace uncertainty, to remain forever open to newness—outwardly and inwardly, physically and spiritually. At birth, a lifetime of adventure beckons. Initially, most of us focus on the tasks at hand: establishing an identity, a home, career, relationships, friends, community, and security, all foundational for getting started in life. If we have good health and financial means, we add travel to the mix. Later in life, many focus increasingly on the inward journey. However, the sooner and the more authentically we live out our spirituality, the better the results.

Our society is deeply divided, not only by politics, race, gender, lifestyle, culture, region, country of origin, social standing, and economic status, but also by religion. When Americans of different faiths disagree, they tend to distrust one another, and even conservatives and liberals of the same denomination are known to regard one another as ignorant, misguided, or diseased. I use that last word intentionally, for people across the denominational spectrum often view those theologically different from themselves—even fellow Christians—as possessing a dangerous and potentially contagious virus destined to bring America to ruin.

Religion, the one factor capable of restoring harmony, unity, and vitality, seems the most divisive and flawed. Designed as a vehicle of hope and grace, religion is being used today to vilify those with alternative lifestyles and views: Protestants versus Catholics, conservatives versus liberals, fundamentalists versus progressives, religionists versus secularists, devout versus nones, literalists versus metaphorists, believers versus atheists, saved versus lost.

Entry 2: The Dualist Dilemma, Part II

Duality thinking, also called polarity thinking or all-or-nothing think-ing, is the bane of spirituality. More than with any other personality trait in our lives, all-or-nothing thinking causes huge mistakes and bad judgments. It results in withholding love, misinterpreting situations, and hurting both others and ourselves. This pattern of dualistic or polarity thinking is deeply entrenched in most of us, despite its severe limitations. Dualistic thinking is not wrong or bad in itself—in fact, it is necessary in most situations. However, it is completely inadequate for the major ques-tions and dilemmas of life.

In *The Heart of Centering Prayer*, American theologian and contem-plative teacher Cynthia Bourgeault presents three approaches that help clarify what Western Christians mean by nonduality:

1. The simplest and most straightforward approach to nonduality is to view it as a person's capacity to bear paradox and ambiguity. Viewed practically, dualistic thinking is characterized by insistence on either/ or, reductionist solutions to life's dilemmas. By contrast, nondual thinking designates the capacity to hold the tension in opposites with-out the need for resolution. According to Bourgeault, the capacity to tolerate paradox and ambiguity represents only a preliminary phase of nonduality, confined to rationality, and while this capacity marks an advancement in basic psychological and moral development, it is only the first step to spiritual nondualism.

2. Another approach equates nonduality with mystical experience, much like "seeing heaven in a grain of sand" or in the sense of finding oneself at one with everything. The problem with this approach, as with most mystical experiences, is that this unitive realization tends to be temporary. In addition, people interpret intuitions of oneness according to the stage of consciousness they have attained. The apostle Paul is a classic example, his extraordinary sense of being "taken up into heaven" coexisting with harshly dualistic pronouncements such as "women should keep silent in church."

3. What if nondual mystical experiences were to continue indefinitely in a permanent state of consciousness? This assumption defines a third major approach to nonduality, for it points to a level of spiritual attainment classically known as "the unitive state." Here we think of

Western mystics such as Julian of Norwich, Meister Eckhart, Teresa of Ávila, and John of the Cross. In Eastern traditions, such experience tends to be monistic, meaning that one's deepest essence or nature is viewed as identical with Ultimate Oneness, whereas in the West, the unitive state is viewed as relational, more like a mystical marriage whereby one is joined to God in love. Here one does not become God, for nondual realization is one of union ("two become one"), not identity. In Western spirituality, humans are made in God's image; we are in God, and God is in us, but we are not God.[1]

However, what if this "close but not identical" approach is more a shift in perception, a level of consciousness rather than actual nondual attainment, a shift not primarily in *what* we see but in *how* we see? This allows us to look at the concept or experience of nonduality not through the lens of spiritual attainment, but through the lens of continuing evolution of consciousness. At this level of consciousness, we see oneness because we see from oneness.

Because the discussion of nonduality contains serious misconceptions, it might be helpful to use a via negative approach to nonduality, clarifying what nonduality does not mean. Nonduality does not and should not remove our capacity for critical thinking. Nondualism does not suspend the head, but rather anchors the head in the deeper ground of the heart, situating it somewhere deeper than in the realm of abstraction and intellect.

Furthermore, Christian nonduality is not the same as philosophical monism, a Hindu tradition that stipulates that because all beings and things begin in the One, all return to the One. This perspective views complexity and differentiation as *maya*, namely, as part of the illusions of the material world. While this perception is certainly nondual, Christian nondualists posit an essential metaphysical difference between materiality and spirituality. The two are not synonymous. It is still possible to look upon the world from a nondual vantage point and affirm the reality of change, evolution, distinction, and uniqueness. According to Western nonduality, one simply sees situations, persons, and things from the perspective of oneness. There is no implicit need to reduce multiplicity to a primal unity in order to lay claim to nondual perception. Even some schools of Hinduism suggest that the unitive state is "not one, not two, but

1. Bourgeault, *Centering Prayer*, 43–52.

both one and two." This, then, is Western nondualism, a way of seeing that is "both/and" rather than exclusively "either/or."

Entry 3: Our Brain's Binary Lens

There is a common belief that human brains are hardwired to think in binary or dualistic ways. The ubiquity of digital computers, coupled with smart phones, nanotechnology, and the rise of artificial intelligence, seems to confirm this way of thinking about the brain, since technological forms of intelligence are related to binary code sequencing, meaning they store data and perform calculations using only zeros and ones. Hence, according to Boolean logic, a single binary digit can only represent True (1) or False (0).

Binary thinking, also known as dichotomous thinking, happens when concepts, ideas, and problems are simplified into being true or false. Other options, such as gray areas in the middle, are ignored or go unnoticed. Binary thinking is useful in situations of threat or danger, when instant decisions are required. Even when humans are not under direct or perceived threat, binary thinking provides a sense of certainty. Such thinking is particularly useful regarding identity, and is a factor affecting gender, race, culture, social class, and religious belief.

While binary applications help us understand certain types of digital computation, the analogy between digital computers and the brain is often misleading. While spiking neurons in the brain may be binary at base, human nervous systems also contain neurons with graded responses. While action potentials are usually binary, synoptic communication between neurons in neural pathways are essentially not binary. Most synapses work by neurotransmitters, meaning they provide chemically mediated graded response. Thus, while neural action potentials are often binary, communication between neurons most often is not binary, since potential firing can involve the integration of synoptic information from many different neurons. Viewed in this way, the brain as a whole cannot be reduced to a binary system, though not all experts agree.

For example, John von Neumann, the famous computer scientist, addressed this idea in his book, *The Computer & the Brain*. Focusing on the behavior of neurons to either fire or not fire, he landed on the side of the brain being a binary system. While that is an important observation, particularly significant for people trying to create artificial brains within computer systems, it is clear that whatever definitions one chooses to work with in terms of brain input and output will affect the outcome. However, the brain within a living human being cannot be reduced to a binary system, for to do so overlooks the comprehensive nature of the human brain, including the interaction between personality, emotions, upbringing, education, experience, and spirituality. In terms of artificial intelligence, any degree of inaccuracy in the starting state of the binary system will cause the behavior of that system to diverge completely from the behavior of the specific brain being modeled. Hence, it is reasonable to conclude that on the macro scale, no particular human brain can be reduced to a binary system, for no binary thinking is final.

Entry 4: Overcoming Dualism, Part I

How does one overcome dualism? How does one awaken to nondualistic awareness? If you have read this far, you deserve to know. The answer, of course, has been there all along.

Life is grand—a gift of nature, society, and family, but above all, of our Creator. As we age, we look backward, nostalgically, idealistically: the highs seem higher, and the lows smaller and shallower. And that's the way it should be. For we are blessed, and our backward glance should be filled with gratitude, not with regret.

Human existence is filled with mental and emotional tension, much of it caused by conflict and polarity. In fact, one cannot live without conflict, and the secret of life is learning to embrace and somehow reconcile one's polarities. To do so successfully requires spirituality. Without spirituality, human beings find themselves trapped in cycles of boredom, irritation, and discontent. By spirituality, I don't mean religion, though they are related.

Speaking of polarities, we need to distinguish them from dualistic thinking, a feature in human consciousness manifested in conventional religious thought. Unlike polarities evident in logic and morality, dualistic thinking refers to a mindset that perceives reality as divided into opposing metaphysical entities such as good versus evil, spirit versus matter, and God versus Satan. Nondualist or holistic thinking does accept the existence of opposites or distinctions in nature, such as maleness and femaleness, lightness and darkness, active and passive, but they are viewed on a continuum and thus, as interrelated.

This ultimate relatedness of all things in the universe is best exempli-fied by the striking Eastern concept called the Tao (pronounced dhow), which speaks of "the way" of reality, the orderly movement of the natural world according to the principle of yin and yang. This is best depicted by the famous Chinese symbol of a circle divided by a backward or reverse S into light and dark (or red and yellow) areas. According to Daoist teaching, yin is the negative force in nature. Understood as passive, it is seen in darkness, coolness, dampness, and femaleness, and is represented by earth, specifically by the moon. Yang is the positive force in nature. Understood as active, it is seen in lightness, warmth, dryness, maleness, and is represented by heaven, specifically by the sun.

All things are on a continuum between yin and yang. For instance, all males have some yin, and all females some yang. These forces are not confined to humans, nor are they static. A rotting tree is said to be losing yang and becoming damp and therefore more yin. No value judgment is given to yin and yang, for neither is better than the other, and neither is solely good or solely evil. Except for a few objects, such as the sun and the earth, which in their totality are yin or yang, the rest of nature, and even events, are a combination. When the two forces work together in harmony, life is as it should be.

Because human brains are hardwired to think in binary or dualistic ways, religious scholar Cantwell Smith distinguished between "conflict dualism" and "complementary dualism." In ancient Mesopotamia, as evident in Zoroastrianism and Manicheism, we find the ideology of conflict dualism, where opposites such as good and evil or God and Satan are locked in constant war. Such ideas influenced Judaism, Christianity, and Islam, based on Greek and Western logic, in which opposites cannot be reconciled. Eastern logic, as exemplified in Taoism and certain forms of Hinduism and Buddhism, emphasizes complementary dualism (nondualist thinking).

The brilliant word, nonduality (*advaita* in Sanskrit), is used by many different traditions, both Eastern and Western, to distinguish from monism, a perspective that erases all diversity and difference, reducing all things to one sameness. Nondualism celebrates difference and affirms diversity. It simply refuses to see this diversity as anything other than the greater unity of a singular Reality.

When referring to nondualism, Cantwell Smith spoke of complementary dualism, but the underlying reality is the same. In nature, things appear as opposites not to conflict with one another but rather to complement each other. In everything they see, think, and experience, nondualists find the dimension of the other.

C. S. Lewis seems to have had this in mind when he identified universal truths in concepts such as the Tao (the Way) in ancient China and *rita* (divine Law or Truth) in early Hinduism.[2] In Hinduism, *rita* is the principle of natural order that regulates and coordinates the operation of the universe and everything in it. Likewise the Chinese speak of the Tao as the essence of reality or the Way of the universe. The ancient Jews conceived of Torah as way, truth, and life. The author of the gospel of John seems to allude to this notion of a universal principle of natural order when he speaks of Jesus as the Logos (the divine Word) in John 1:1, 14 and as the Way, the Truth, and the Life in 14:6.

Entry 5: Overcoming Dualism, Part II

Nondualism is not monism. Monism reduces all things to the same thing, erasing all diversity and difference. Nondualism celebrates difference and affirms diversity. It simply refuses to see this diversity as anything other than the greater unity of a singular Reality. As contemplatives have always known and modern-day ecology and quantum physics is only now discovering, all things in nature are both metaphysically distinct and one at the same time. Nondualistic thinking or "third-eye" seeing is not a technique for acquiring things, a pious exercise that makes God happy, or a requirement for entry into heaven. It is more like practicing heaven now. Such experience is invariably the same—relinquishing particularity, one's sense of separate self, to an egoless awareness that leaves one with an unshakeable sense that all is God.

Our ultimate fascination, of course, is with the world within, exploring the limits and possibilities of our humanity, individually and corporately. The ultimate adventure, the grandest game, the greatest challenge, is the spiritual transformation of the self. The following parable, adapted from Mark 10:17–31 and 8:34–38, helps illustrate the level of passion and commitment necessary for spiritual transformation to occur. One day, as Jesus and his disciples approached Jericho on their way to Jerusalem, Jesus paused at the Jordan River, removed his sandals and tunic, and entered the

2. Lewis, *Abolition of Man*, 27–29. In an appendix, "Illustrations of the Tao," Lewis examines eight examples of the Natural Law found in legal and religious texts across cultures of antiquity, 95–121.

water, welcoming newcomers by baptism. A young man stepped from the crowd, and standing at the bank of the river, addressed Jesus.

"Good Teacher," he said, "what must I do to inherit eternal life?" And Jesus replied, "Why do you connect eternal life with doing? Eternal life is more a matter of being than doing."

The young man answered, "I was brought up to believe that God would not accept me unless I was a good person. Hence, I have kept all the moral commandments. All my life I have sought wealth and success," he continued, "and have attained them. I believe I am a good person. Others admire me, and I have tried to be a model citizen, paying my taxes, giving my tithe to the synagogue, and giving alms to the poor. But something is lacking, and I sense I am too selfish, too possessive, and too self-assured. I am fearful of losing what I have achieved, and fearful of strangers, of change, of letting go. I am struggling with racism, sexism, and homophobia, and I fear I am succumbing to entitlement, exceptionalism, and white supremacy. Despite my social success, I feel morally inadequate and spiritually immature. Can you help me?"

And Jesus, looking at him, loved him, and said, "Enter the water and come to me." The young man did as Jesus commanded, and as he drew near to Jesus, the latter said, "Will you trust me?"

Nodding assent, the young man presented himself for baptism. Placing his hands on the young man's shoulders, Jesus gently nudged him into the water. Taking a deep breath and trusting Jesus, the young man felt his upper body engulfed by water. Under the water, he felt relaxed and confident. However, after a while, running short of air, he struggled upward, only to encounter pressure downward. Jesus seemed to be fighting him, holding him under. He relaxed further, knowing he could survive a few seconds longer. Finally, frantic and desperate for air, he struggled with all his might, and only then did Jesus relinquish his forcible hold.

Unfazed, Jesus embraced him while saying, "If you seek eternal life— if you desire spiritual transformation—you must want it as desperately as you cling to your own mortal life, and even more. If you wish to be my disciple, you must deny yourself and follow me. For those who want to save their life will lose it, and those who lose their life for my sake, and for the sake of the gospel, will save it. Young man, you are too self-assured: give up your pride, your accomplishments, your prejudice, your sense of supremacy, and your fear of change; then come, follow me." And the young man did as Jesus said.

Then Jesus looked around and said to his disciples, "How hard it is for those who are successful and self-assured to enter the kingdom. It is easier for a cable to go through the eye of a needle than for someone who is self-obsessed to enter the kingdom of God." His disciples were greatly astounded and said to one another, "Then who can be saved?" Jesus looked at them and said, "For mortals, personal transformation is impossible, but not for God; for God all things are possible."

This parable, a modern adaptation of Jesus' encounter with the rich young man, addresses many of the problems in our world today. Our planet is unhealthy, our civilization fragile, our nation overly hostile, our communities vulnerable, and our neighborhoods unsafe. American corporations are too greedy and immoral, and American citizens too fearful, impulsive, and self-obsessed. To change our planet, we must change global civilization; to change our world, we must change our nation; to change America, we must change our communities; and to change our neighborhoods, we must change ourselves, beginning with you and me.

Global health begins with social transformation, and social transformation with personal transformation. Personal transformation begins with self-reflection, sincerity, honesty, integrity, and right intent. Before we humans can change, we must discover our need for change—what the mystics in our religious traditions call "awareness" or "awakeness"—and desire transformation as desperately as the air we breathe.

Levels of Meaning

Entry 1: Four Paths to Meaning

FROM TIME IMMEMORIAL, IN every age, nation, culture, and society, a set of questions has persisted, perplexing human beings. Who am I? Why am I here? Where did I come from? Where am I going? They have been called life's existential questions; philosophers speak of them as "ultimate questions," for they are the ones that never go away.

While we know there are no final or absolute answers to existential questions, they must be asked, especially early in life. At some point we realize that the answers, however given or explained, are not as important as the questions. Nevertheless, the questions must be asked, if for no other reason that they have an integrative function, helping individuals learn how to process information, how to conceptualize, how to interact with others, and how to understand themselves and their place in the grand scheme of life.

As we age physically and progress morally, emotionally, and intellectually, we discover four paths to meaning. To simplify, we can list and rank them as follows:

1. literal or factual

2. symbolic or metaphorical

3. allegorical or parabolic

4. mythological or mystical

As is clear, the most superficial and therefore least effective level of knowing is the factual or literal. We cannot downplay this level, for it is the foundation upon which the first half of life is built. A factual understanding of an event or a discipline is a doorway. Such an approach gets us in the ballpark of thinking, understanding, and living, but it remains superficial. Shallow knowledge gives us confidence, like a child going ankle deep at the beach or wearing floaties in a pool, but it is not swimming. Such knowledge can lead to arrogance and deception. Perhaps you have heard others indicate how, when they read a book, heard a lecture, or attended a seminar, they thought they knew a great deal, only to read additional books or hear other points of view and discover how little they knew about the subject. If you've had this experience, you have something in common with Einstein, who acknowledged, "The more I learn, the more I realize how much I don't know."

Entry 2: Four Points of View

As we know, people are divided morally, epistemologically, cosmologically, politically, and religiously by competing points of view. On the one hand are those who focus on absolutes, opposed by those who argue for progress and change. Others, noting the dualistic impasse between polarities, argue for synthesis, seeking compromise as a solution. This is what Franciscans mean when they call their movement "alternative orthodoxy," a heterodoxy somewhere between conformity and nonconformity on the theological spectrum, or what the eminent biologist Theodosius Dobzhansky meant when he wrote, "I am a creationist *and* an evolutionist."

Do these three options exhaust the possibilities? Is another alternative possible, a quaternary point of view? There is a fourth alternative, one espoused by sages, mystics, and saints throughout history. In the Bible, we find the fourth face of God in YHWH, in the "I Am" of God, the unspeakable absolute oneness of God (see Exod 3:14). This is the face of God that, according to Exodus 33:20, no one can see and live, the God we know through unknowing. This is why there are four ways of reading scripture (literal, tropological [moral meaning], allegorical, and anagogical [eschatological meaning]) or according to Lectio Divina, four ways of praying scripture (*lectio, meditatio, oratio,* and *contemplatio*), why nature has four seasons (spring, summer, fall, and winter), and why a deck of cards is composed of four suits (hearts, diamonds, spades, and clubs). It is also what Hinduism means by four paths to God (the path of works, devotion, knowledge, and self-actualization); what Jesus meant by loving God with our heart, soul, mind, and strength, (which correlates with feeling, intuition, thinking, and sensing, the four functions of personality used by the Swiss psychiatrist Carl

G. Jung and later utilized by the Myers Briggs Type Indicator [MBTI] to determine personality type); what John F. Haught calls the four components of wholesome religion (sacramental, mystical, silent, and active); what Peter Tufts Richardson calls the four spirituality types (the journey of works, devotion, unity, and harmony); what theologian Brian McLaren calls the four stages of faith (simplicity, complexity, perplexity, and harmony); what Urban Holmes calls four schools of spirituality (sacramental, charismatic, mystical, and apostolic); or what Cynthia Bourgeault means when she suggests that we replace binary systems of understanding with ternary perspectives, such as are present in the Christian Trinity. In this case, the third force is not a product of the first two, as in the classic Hegelian synthesis, but is independent and coequal with the others.

According to Bourgeault, the interweaving of the three forces produces a fourth realm of possibility. In contrast to binary systems, which seek completion in stability, through the balance of opposites, ternary perspectives create a synthesis at a completely new level, seeking completion in newness. In *The Holy Trinity and the Law of Three*, Bourgeault advises that we not limit this metaphysical principle to one triad (Father, Son, and Holy Spirit), but rather that we envision the Holy Trinity as one of many triads, each revealing different facets of the divine wholeness. Such a way of conceptualizing is made easier if we stop thinking of the doctrine of the Trinity as about three *persons* and envision it in terms of metaphysical *process*, as three functions or forces rather than three identities. The result is not a compromise, like changing the score in a ballgame, but what Bourgeault calls "an arising," namely, a completely new ballgame.

Most of Christianity's metaphysical paradigms are binary systems. For example, to think of God in masculine or feminine categories is to reduce reality to paired opposites. Ternary systems, however, present a distinctly different mix. The interplay of two polarities calls forth a third, thereby generating synthesis at an entirely new level, which results in new realms of possibility. Think of the agricultural process of planting and sowing. A seed, as Jesus said, "unless it falls into the ground and dies, it remains just a single grain" (John 12:24). If *seed* (the first force) meets *ground* (the second force), which must be moist, nothing happens without a third or reconciling force, *sunlight*. When these three forces interact, they generate a *sprout*, which is the actualization of the possibility latent in the seed. Unlike binary systems, ternary systems are not about paired opposites but about threefold process, which leads to new fields of possibility, because the fourth force is not a final and stable completion but "the new arising that inevitably emerges from the dynamic interplay of the three."[1]

Is it possible to utilize all four levels of consciousness simultaneously? Yes, because spirituality enables and encourages such plasticity. According to mystics and sages, humans consist of body, mind, soul (heart and emotions), and spirit. Don't we humans live out of our fourfold nature simultaneously?

Entry 3: Levels of Reality, Part I

In his 1976 book, *Forgotten Truth*, the renowned scholar of comparative religions, Huston Smith, delves into the Perennial Tradition, the common, fundamental experience of humankind as found in the core teachings of the world's religions, identifying therein a cosmology based on the idea of an ontological gradation of reality.

According to Smith, perennial wisdom is perhaps best distinguished by its recognition of the many-layered nature of both reality and the self. Smith narrows these layers to four: reality is composed of the terrestrial, intermediate, celestial, and infinite levels, while the self is composed of the body, mind, soul, and spirit.

These tiers correlate in such a way that higher levels of reality correspond to deeper levels of the self:

- The terrestrial tier (also called the material, physical, sensible, corporeal, and phenomenal) corresponds to the body.

- The intermediate tier (also called the subtle, psychic, or astral) corresponds to the mind.

- The celestial tier (this realm views God as personal; here one speaks of God's attributes and personality) corresponds to the soul.

- The Infinite tier (this realm views God as transpersonal; this level is best spoken of through analogy, in negative terms, or through paradox) corresponds to the Spirit.

Smith's cosmological image shows the earth, symbolic of the terrestrial sphere, enveloped by the intermediate sphere, which in turn is enclosed by the celestial, the three concentric spheres together superimposed on a background that represents the Infinite. "Considered in itself, each sphere

1. Bourgeault, *Holy Trinity*, 19.

appears as a complete and homogeneous whole, while from the perspective of the area that encloses and permeates it, it is but a content. Thus the terrestrial world knows not the intermediate world, or the latter the celestial, though each world is known and dominated by the one that exceeds and enfolds it."[2] With each higher level, different laws apply, together with a different way of experiencing reality. The highest and deepest tiers, Infinite and Spirit, are, according to Smith, without limitation; while the Infinite is unbounded externally, the human Spirit is unbounded internally. These two levels, therefore, are in fact the same.

Entry 4: Levels of Reality, Part II

As one moves down Smith's tiers of reality and out the tiers of selfhood, one encounters increasing levels of differentiation and/or materialization. In the primordial tradition, the possibility exists that one of the higher metaphysical levels can "break through" into one of the lower levels, in so doing overriding the laws of that lower level. While religion explores all four levels holistically, the laws of science are limited in their application primarily to the physical (terrestrial) level.

Whereas Smith places the body in the innermost circle, as the most accessible aspect, with the other levels expanding concentrically outward to the spirit, humanity's most expansive element, I think of the body as the outermost level, the container for the inner levels of selfhood. I begin with the body and emphasize its role for two reasons: (a) to counter longstanding religious misrepresentations of the body as the place and cause of sin, and (b) to highlight the body's vital role in spiritual health. One of the great tragedies of religious history occurred when the physical body was falsely accused for the sins of humanity. The idea that our most basic bodily functions, including our sensual pleasure and sexual passion, are unclean and unholy is not only a regrettable belief system, it is also profoundly ignorant. In her book *The Seeker's Guide*, Elizabeth Lesser affirms that "[d]eep spirituality is not an out-of-body experience; it's an in-body experience."[3]

Body and mind are not separate; neither are body and emotions or body and soul. Humans are not spiritual beings trapped in a carnal existence. The self is like a diamond, each part a facet of the same essence. When we view our bodies as base and vulgar and our souls and spirits as pure and distinct,

2. Smith, *Forgotten Truth*, 61.
3. Lesser, *Seeker's Guide*, 242.

we affirm dualism, the bane of spirituality. If we recognize our bodies to be "materialized spirit," and therefore spiritually based, we are on our way to wholeness and truth. Care of the body, therefore, is the first and most important principle of religion. If we are to make spiritual progress, we must learn to love and care for our bodies. The physical is the doorway to the spiritual. This is the starting premise of all healthy spirituality.

Moving inward from body we come to mind, the seat of consciousness, conceived as distinct from the brain, which is part of the body. The mind is not our thoughts, but rather a container for life's continual creative impulses. According to Smith, there is no convincing materialistic explanation of mind, for mind cannot be measured quantitatively. Furthermore, mind conforms to laws that differ in kind from those that matter exemplifies.

The third level of selfhood is the soul (called by ancients *psyche, anima, atman, nephesh,* or *nafs*), the final locus of our individuality, its source and yet superior. The soul is closer to our essence than is the mind, with which we usually identify. While the soul is finite, it is the only possible bridge to Spirit, the fourth level of selfhood. If soul is the element in humans that relates to God, Spirit is the element that is identical with God, not with God's personal mode but with God's mode that is infinite. Mystics and theologians speak of identity at this level because here the subject-object dichotomy is transcended." While Spirit is infinite, humans remain finite because they are not Spirit only. Our specifically human overlay—body, mind, and soul—is said to veil the Spirit within us.

The key point in Smith's model is the realization that as far as selfhood is concerned, one cannot maintain harmony, equilibrium, and flow by jumping across levels. Each level builds consecutively and concentrically on the preceding. In other words, the bridge to consciousness is the body. To understand the mind, one must be fully grounded in one's physicality. The link to soul is mind, and the link to Spirit is soul. Each level must be explored deeply and authentically before it can serve as conduit to the next. To acquire meaning and understanding, one cannot jump from body to soul or from mind to Spirit. For Smith, the final link, the door that leads from soul to spirit, is love: "For Spirit to permeate the self's entirety, the components of the self must be aligned: body in temperance, mind in understanding, and soul in love."[4]

---

4. Smith, *Forgotten Truth*, 92.

Entry 5: Moving Toward Wisdom

When most of us think of faith, we think of it as a noun, that is, as a body of belief. In spirituality, however, faith is first a verb before it becomes a noun, a way of trusting and living before it becomes a way of believing. Unfortunately, most of us reverse that equation. We start with belief, and then we try to act accordingly. That approach only lasts so long before it collapses from failure, inertia, or exertion. To discover the truth, we must become the truth. First, we must act, and then we will understand. That is the mysterious wisdom of faith. Called the "primacy of action," it is the wisdom we learn only when we are on the way. This is a lesson nobody can teach us; we must go down this road ourselves. This is the place of the soul, the place of wisdom, toward which we must move. In the end, truth is an encounter much more than a concept that can be argued. We are realigned with truth when the real person meets the real God, which is exactly the stuff of spirituality, theology, and conversion.

There are two necessary paths enabling us to move toward wisdom: a radical journey inward and a radical journey outward. For too long we have confined people to a sort of secure middle position, a safe midpoint between these two great teachers. Failure and falling short are the best teachers; success has practically nothing to teach on the spiritual path. Through education or by temperament, most of us fall into one of two camps, mysticism (the focus is inward) or activism (the focus is outward). Unfortunately, these two types seldom come together, and thus they both miss half the truth.

The great temptation of Western Christians has been to imprison the gospel in their heads. Up there, one can be right or wrong, a position correct or false, but in any case, everything must remain firmly under one's control. On the other hand, action never allows the illusion of control, at least not for long. For this reason alone, it seems obvious that we must begin primarily with action.

In *Walking on Water* I describe a path based on unfailing vision and enduring truth. Exploring ideas common to the Perennial Tradition[5] and the Judeo-Christian heritage, *Walking on Water* helps us become wise at the deepest level, living harmoniously with ourselves, others, the earth, and the Creator. The following ideas summarize that book:

5. The Perennial Tradition is discussed in topic 10 below.

1. The goodness of God fills all the gaps of the universe, without discrimination or preference. The space between everything is not space at all but God's Spirit.

2. Death is not just physical dying, but hitting bottom, going the distance beyond when the ego is in control, fully beyond what I am now. Grace is found at the depths and in the death of everything. After these smaller deaths, the only "deadly sin" is to swim on the surface of things, where we never see, find, or desire God and love. This includes even the surface of religion, which might be the worst danger of all.

3. When we go into the full depths and death, even the depths of our own sin, we come out the other side—and the word for that is resurrection. None of us crosses over by our own effort or merits, purity or perfection. We are all carried across by unearned grace. The tomb is always finally empty. There are no exceptions to death, and there are no exceptions to grace or resurrection.

Topic 10

Perennial Wisdom

Entry 1: Introduction

THE CURRENT GENERATION OUTPACES all others in history in terms of wealth, health, education, and convenience—yet it doesn't seem to be happier or more content than preceding generations. Perhaps, in our passion for acquiring things, we have actually lost something profound—something so valuable that we would never knowingly sell it or trade it away. Some may refer to values, standards, or patriotism, but what it comes down to is the loss of the sacred.

Rather than being rooted in a spiritual worldview and in principles espoused by the traditions of the world's great religions, particularly in their mystical approaches to reality, modern humans see the world through the lenses of crass materialism, scientism, and positivism. In his thoughtful volume, *Man and Nature: the Spiritual Crisis in Modern Man* (1997), Islamic scholar Seyyed Nasr takes the reader through history and explores the causes of the desacralization of nature in the West and the resultant ecological crisis we face today. He demonstrates how the West, by divorcing science from spirit, has wreaked havoc on our planet. He also argues that the Christian faith helped accelerate this process when it removed elements of its metaphysical doctrines that kept nature as a part of the divine.

Given the quandary we face, socially and environmentally, exacerbated by our complicity with racism and our propensity for exploiting natural resources, America needs help. Ironically, if solutions exist, they must come not from exclusively American expertise—from uniquely modern, scientific, or Christian values—but from the Perennial Tradition, from peoples, beliefs, and customs North Americans have traditionally overlooked, discarded, or displaced in their strident surge onward.

When I speak of the Perennial Tradition, sometimes called Perennial Philosophy or simply "the wisdom tradition," I am referring to the view that the world's major religions share common teachings, and that these truths transcend culture, time, and place. Jews, Christians, or members of any specific religion, should not feel they were the first to know God's eternal patterns and presence. After all, those patterns are perfectly plain, because God has made it plain. "Ever since the creation of the world [God's] eternal power and divine nature, invisible though they are, have been understood and seen through the things [God] has made" (Rom 1:19–20). How else could it be? How could any God worthy of the name squeeze Being itself into any specific timeframe, culture, or vocabulary? That is what we mean by the Perennial Tradition.

People who value perennial wisdom share core existential questions with other human beings, only they do not confine their search for answers to any one religion. What I call "core existential questions," what philosophers call "ultimate questions," can be reduced to four: (1) "Is there an ultimate reality?" (2) "Can I relate to that reality?" (3) "How does that relationship affect the way I live?" and (4) "What can I hope for?" Because these questions never go away, they form the heart of almost every spiritual quest.

It is the main business of religion to answer life's existential questions. A useful place to start is the Perennial Tradition, by which I mean not the distinct perspectives of other religious traditions—for the goal of spiritual transformation is a deeper understanding of one's own faith tradition, not conversion to some alternative religious tradition—but rather the congruence of values and beliefs (absolutes) across cultures, those unchanging beliefs that unite human traditions that seek wisdom in ancient texts and modes of life. According to perennial wisdom, every religious tradition, when one explores its mystical side, articulates common answers to humanity's existential questions, answers that emerge repeatedly throughout human history and across human culture.

Entry 2: Divine Reality

Perennial wisdom, found in most human cultures, religions, and civilizations, begins not with time, space, matter, or even with ontology (speculation about divine essence or Being), but with a common singularity we call Unity, or better yet, Mystery. As Lao Tzu, the sixth-century BCE author of the *Tao Te Ching*, says in his opening poem, "The Tao that can be named is not the eternal Tao. The name that can be named is not the eternal name . . . Darkness within darkness. The gate to all mystery."

The Perennial Tradition says that there is a capacity for divine reality inside all humans, but we initially cannot see what we are looking for because what we are looking for is doing the looking. God, the name most of us give to Ultimate Reality, is never an object to be found or possessed as we find other objects, but the One who shares our deepest subjectivity by virtue of being only Subject, never object.

Dualistic people use knowledge, even religious knowledge, for the purposes of ego enhancement, shaming, and the control of others and themselves, for it works very well in that way. Nondual people use knowledge for the transformation of persons and structures, but especially to experience transformation, seeing reality with a new eye and heart.

This realization helps to explain the great paradox we all must face—and embrace—that God is both perfectly hidden and perfectly revealed in all things. God has written the pattern in things as they are, and yet we never see the full pattern without divine assistance. Thus, faith (trust in the divine) is always necessary to see what is "natural."

In the context of comparative religion, it is wrong to claim that all Gods are the same, or that all Gods are variations of a specific context. If you want to study Allah, study Islam. If you want to learn about Krishna, Vishnu, Shiva, and the rest of the Gods of India, study the many schools of Hinduism. In the study of world religions, each deity must be allowed to speak in its own way, or at least to reflect the values of its priests, prophets, sages, and gurus.

The Perennial Tradition, however, does not seek such distinctions. Rather, it sifts through the scriptures and teachings of many cultures looking for those teachings that transcend the limits of specific cultures and point to the Reality that cannot be named, defined, or figured out. Augustine, the great fifth-century theologian, articulated that very idea when he declared, *"Si comprehenderis, non est Deus"* (If you understand, then what you understand is not God). God, it seems, cannot really be known, but only related to.

Such teaching, central to scripture, is regularly overlooked by people committed to religious uniqueness or denominational distinctives. Due to scripture's narrative nature, essential teachings about God are not dealt with abstractly, dogmatically, or systematically, but rather in pastoral or social settings, such as by caring for the poor and needy (Jer 22:16) and by loving fellow human beings in general (1 John 4:20; see also James 1:27).

Is the Perennial Tradition, the perspective that all the world's religions share a single truth or origin, consonant with Christianity? For many, this perspective is false, misleading, and heretical. For others, however, it is not only compatible with Christianity, but it represents an essential and oft overlooked aspect of Christianity, perhaps its deepest insight and teaching.

Entry 3: Global Citizenship: A Profound Commitment to Nature, Part I

The central defining characteristic of spirituality is an individual's sense of connection to a much greater whole. At its heart, spirituality involves an emotional experience of awe and reverence. Such experience is highly desired, fervently sought, endlessly disagreed upon, and thoroughly fascinating.

The world we live in today is the world we know through scientific observation, a much different world from the classical world where Western civilization first emerged. At that time, there was greater continuity between religion, culture, and nature. Today, however, we are experiencing a discontinuity unequaled in its order of magnitude. That is why there is suspicion and misrepresentation among the religions of the present time and why we are experiencing new fundamentalisms: Islamic, Jewish, Christian, Buddhist, Hindu, and Shinto.

Fundamentalism is a defensive tactic. It is one reason why few of the religions of the world are dealing with the ecology issue on a widespread scale. They simply do not feel equipped to deal with this new challenge. By not accepting a responsibility for the fate of the earth, there is a failure of religious responsibility to the divine, as well as to the human. We seem not to realize that as the outer world becomes damaged, our sense of the divine is degraded correspondingly.

Why did our ancestors have such a wonderful idea of God? Because they lived in an awesome world. They wondered at the magnificence of whatever it was that brought the world into being. This led to a sense of adoration. This adoration, this gratitude, we call religion. But now, as the outer world is diminished, our inner world is drying up.

Religion involves the sense of God, of the human, of creation, and of revelation. All of these aspects belong together, and they cannot be treated separately. We would have no sense of the divine without creation. Speculatively, we could talk about God as being prior to or outside creation or independent of creation, but in actual fact there is no such being as God without creation.

Pagans are seen as idolatrous because they worship the forces of nature and depict the divine in natural images and forms. But the divine always appears in some embodiment; no one ever worshiped matter as matter. Whatever is worshiped is seen as a mode of divine presence. Prior to the advent of monotheism, the divine was experienced by peoples generally as an all-pervasive presence of mysterious power in the universe. Biblical people drew together this all-pervasive presence in a transcendent, divine, personal creator related by covenant to a special people. People in the West, who inherited this outlook, gained a great deal, including a historical perspective, a sense of personal identity, and a sense of community. But they gradually lost the outer world, and when the outer world is lost, much of the inner world is lost as well.

Christianity allows for both the immanence and transcendence of God. The two polarities, however, must be maintained in tension. Excessive emphasis on the immanence of God can limit the divine to the range of purely natural phenomena. Excessive emphasis on the transcendence of God, however, can lead to apathy toward nature or even to misuse of its resources, thereby contributing to the destruction of the planet.

Of course, we have to recognize that immanence—this divine presence in creation—is understood differently in our present historical context than by our primal ancestors. Primal peoples related to nature immediately and intuitively; they simply observed and admired the natural world about them. Time was eternal—it moved in ever-renewing, seasonal cycles of change—and the universe existed as it always was and always would be. Humans could not really interfere with that or change it.

In the biblical world, however, a new sense of history came into being, an awareness that the universe emerged into being at a definite moment. Modern science, though it perceives the universe through a different set of intellectual lenses, with the aid of microscopic and telescopic instruments, reinforces the biblical perspective. Gradually, the Western world has come to understand that the universe is not simply a given, and that it did indeed have a beginning in time. And time, we have discovered, is irreversible. Our modern scientific view of the universe thus coincides with the biblical realm rather than with the non-biblical world.

Entry 4: Global Citizenship: A Profound Commitment to Nature, Part II

There is something very important about the origin of the universe as we now know it. The beginning of the universe, we now understand, involved articulated energy constellations bound together in an inseparable unity. The various parts of the universe, while outwardly differentiated, were once inwardly bonded together in a comprehensive intimacy of each particle with every other particle.

Ecotheologian Thomas Berry indicates that at the beginning of the universe there were two forces: an expansive force, which resulted in a diversification process, and an attractive or gravitational force, which pulled things together in profound intimacy. While this attraction that everything has for everything else is vital, nobody knows its nature. Isaac Newton (1642–1727), who noted the laws of gravitation, said he did not know what gravitation was, and to this day no one can tell us what gravitation is. But we do know that these antithetical forces, the attractive force and the explosive force, together constitute what is called the curvature of the universe. According to Berry, "Everything that exists comes into existence within this context, the curvature of space. If this rate of emergence had been a trillionth of a fraction faster or a trillionth of a fraction slower, the universe would have either exploded or collapsed . . . If the attraction overcame the expansion, it would collapse. But if the expansion overcame the attraction, then it would explode."[1] Gravitation, built into this process, binds everything together so closely that nothing can ever be separated from anything else. Alienation, therefore, of one human from another or of humans from nature, is only a perception, for it is a cosmological impossibility.

As Berry points out, the other thing that is so important to this process is the relationship of origin: everything in the universe is derived from the same source. Science indicates that, and so does theology. If that is so, then everything in the universe is cousin to everything else. There is literally one family in the universe, one bonding. Community is not something we humans invented. And if the planet is a single community of existence, then all living beings are interconnected and all things are vital. In a universe where everything is related by origin, nothing is unimportant, nothing is marginal.

---

1. Cited in Dunn and Lonergan, *Befriending the Earth*.

The current crisis of humanity is, in essence, a crisis of a lack of relationship. Humans are out of touch with themselves—with one another, with nature, with their past, with their future—but also with the Creator, the God of the universe. As this crisis grows, so does the yearning for relatedness. And that is the good news. Crisis precedes transformation and actually fuels or serves as a catalyst for transformation.

In the journey of life upon which we have all embarked, the most important task is to cultivate a sense of trust. Nothing will serve us better than a profound and ever deepening trust in the Creator, the sovereign power that keeps the vast panorama of universal existence moving along. Yes, the world is in poor shape, and many of its problems grow worse with each passing day. We must do what we can, but we must not fall into despair. If we focus on the big picture, we will realize that the universe is in a continual state of change. And we must remember that our planet is only a small part of the whole, that our crises are but fleeting instants in the eternity of time. There is perfection to the order and flow of this grand universe that is not absent from our tiny earth or our present time.

Entry 5: Recapturing the Sacramental Sense of Reality

John F. Haught, professor of theology at Georgetown University, argues that when it is wholesome, religion maintains four components: sacramental, mystical, silent, and active. Each of these dimensions suggests a distinct "way" of being religious, he argues, "but religion is most healthy and alive when it blends all four ways harmoniously. And it begins to dissolve into something other than 'religion' whenever any of the four aspects is isolated from contact with its three partners. In the actual world of religious life, such sundering of one aspect from the others is not unusual. But when this splintering occurs, religion rapidly decays into magic, escapism or obsession with esoteric teachings, or into cynicism, iconoclasm or vacuous activism."[2] When, on the other hand, religion concretely preserves the four components in a balanced way, it will function in an ecologically supportive way.

What fascinates me most about these aspects is the sacramental dimension. Religion is sacramental in the sense that it can speak of unspeakable mystery only through the use of symbols, or what theology calls sacraments. A sacrament, in its broadest sense, includes any object, person

2. Haught, *Promise of Nature*, 73–75.

or event through which religious consciousness is awakened to the presence of sacred mystery. Historically, most of religion's sacraments have been closely related to nature. For example, the luminosity of sunshine, dawn, and dusk; the experience of wind or breath; the purifying power of clean water; the fertility of soil and life—all of these natural phenomena, and many more, have been used by religions to symbolize the way in which ultimate mystery affects us.

Since nature provides many of the fundamental sacraments of human religion, it is easy to see how the conservation of nature is indispensable for the survival of religion. If we lose the environment, we lose God as well. And it is equally true that when religion loses touch with its sacramental origins, it begins to grow indifferent to the natural world. A sacramental vision, Haught reminds us, makes nature, at least in a fragmentary way, transparent to divinity. In this sense it concedes to nature an inherent value without allowing it to become a substitute for God. According to this Christian perspective, nature is worth saving not because it is sacred, but because it is sacramental.

Of course, religion can exaggerate its sacramental side. It does so when it loses its association with mysticism, its essential polarity, as well as silence and action, another set of opposites that exists in a sort of tension with sacramentalism. When mysticism is lost, the sacrament becomes an end in itself, losing its symbolic value. But mysticism alone, if it diminishes the value of nature by looking exclusively beyond the natural order, can decay into sheer escapism. Occasionally it has even gone to the extreme of hating the earth and everything natural. Mysticism and sacramentalism are necessary, as are silence and action, but they need to be delicately balanced. Mysticism dissociated from a vigorous sacramentalism promotes the doctrine of "cosmic homelessness," whereas sacramentalism without the mystical aspect of religion collapses into idolatry or pure naturalism (the view that nature is all there is).

In his book *The Luminous Dusk*, Professor Dale Allison explores the loss of wonder in Western society and its negative impact on our relationship to the cosmos. Arguing that early Christians favored the desert to the city, finding it natural to practice Christianity in solitude and silence, he laments that modern people forsook the wilderness and filled the cities. As a result, they have lost soul, for the closer humans came to themselves, the more cynical they became.

Allison mentions a poll of scientists taken some years ago, whose object was to gauge their belief in God. Although few acknowledged a belief in God, of those that did, there was a significantly higher percentage of cosmologists than biologists, and a significantly higher percentage of biologists than psychologists. The results led Allison to conclude that the closer one's profession takes one toward human beings, the less belief in God there is.[3]

3. Allison, *Luminous Dusk*, 13.

The Value of Myth

Entry 1: Introduction

WHILE A LITERAL READING of scripture or factual knowledge of religion is a good starting point to spirituality, it is the least effective and least transformative way to live, think, and "know." According to Joseph Campbell, valued in his day as the world's foremost interpreter of mythology, metaphor, whether expressed symbolically, allegorically, or mythologically, is the most suitable language for religion, for it alone is honest about Mystery. "Metaphors only seem to describe the outer world of time and place," he noted; however, "Their real universe is the spiritual realm of the inner life."[1] Authentic religion masters metaphor, transporting from the known to the unknown. Mythology, the most profound and effective level of understanding, certainly the most integrative, helps individuals discover life's meaning in four ways:

1. *Symbolic function.* Mythology influences us subconsciously, helping us approach our questions intuitively, at nonverbal, preconceptual, and pre-emotional levels.

2. *Scholastic function.* Mythology guides individuals through the stages and transitions of life. Mythology's tutorial or explanatory function provides harmonious ways through the inevitable crises of life.

3. *Sociological function.* Mythology supports and validates social order, helping individuals discover their place and role in society.

4. *Synchronous function.* Mythology opens the mind to wonder and the heart to transcendence, pointing out the ultimate mystery in which all

---

1. Campbell, *Thou Art That*, 7.

things participate. Mythology's unifying function links human beings to society, one another, nature, and the cosmos.

Entry 2: The Wasteland

Aristotle said democracy would only work in a culture committed to virtue; Jesus said we must know the truth, for only truth can set us free (John 8:32); the book of Proverbs maintains that where there is no vision, there is no common restraint (29:18). In the past, society was guided by common principles, inspired truth. Today there is no communal myth to guide us, no common vision to inspire us, no transcendent images to shape us.

Given our divisive attitudes and perspectives, a single cultural myth or national story may no longer be possible. Many today are unable to offer one another basic respect, engage in civic dialogue, or honor the human struggle. Modern humans have become adept at dissecting, critiquing, disagreeing, shaming. Despite its ubiquity, however, faultfinding is not an art form. It does not represent the kind of deep passion or positive faith that can stand up to war, vengeance, or injustice.

Human beings need to find that rare ability to live happily in a broken world and still work for its reform. It is a way of living that I believe only spirituality can achieve. Mere ideology is not sufficient for the task. Conservative ideologues, in my opinion, often have no practical goal beyond preserving the status quo, and liberal ideologues no useful objective beyond maintaining personal and social freedom. While this is a generalization, what ideologues often lack is a spiritual center, a reference point beyond the individual "I" or corporate "We." Lacking a God who gives source, pattern, and external goal, they create gods in their own image, becoming their own god. Contrast that to the prophets of old, all claiming an authority beyond their own, a Center outside of themselves.

In the beginning God said, "Let it be," and from that fecund singularity emerged incredible diversity, resulting in a universe filled with galaxies containing trillions of stars. In one such galaxy, called the Milky Way, there evolved on a planet called earth millions of species, one of its species, *homo erectus*, proliferating into astonishing billions of human beings, further dividing into families, tribes, clans, nations, cultures, social classes, races, and religions.

As perception developed, human beings used senses, reason, and experience to divide and separate reality into component parts, using binary categories to categorize and distinguish one thing from another. Primal peoples and children, it seems, retain the ability to think holistically, to intuit and envision the original unity underlying reality, a quality many people recapture in old age. In the interim, however, beginning with puberty and continuing through adolescence and well into adult life, the primal unifying vision, corrupted by fear, stress, insecurity, and the need of security and success, became lost.

That, of course, is the meaning of the Grail, often associated with Christ's passion.[2] According to one Christian version, the Grail was brought from heaven by neutral angels. Envisioning a war in heaven between good and evil, God and Satan, one medieval writer built on biblical imagery to describe how some angelic hosts sided with Satan and others with God. In this sense, the Grail represents the unifying spiritual path between pairs of opposites such as fear and desire and good and evil.

The backdrop to the Grail quest is that the country, the land, indeed the whole territory of concern, has been laid waste. It is what life looks like when reality is viewed dualistically, the spiritual superseding the natural. The nature of this wasteland is a way of living characterized as inauthentic, where people do as they are told, living like those around them, conforming to the status quo, with little courage or imagination to be unique. It is a way of living selfishly, forever climbing the ladder of success, oblivious or immune to the needs and suffering of others. This is what T. S. Eliot spoke of in his poem *The Waste Land*.

Entry 3: The Fisher King

The earliest surviving version of the Grail legend is *Perceval, le Conte del Graal*, composed about 1180 by Chrétien de Troyes, who declared that he adapted the tale from a book given to him by his benefactor Count Philip of Flanders, shortly before the departure of Count Philip for the Holy Land in 1190. The Grail quest, while inclusive and harmonious with the whole, adopts the resources of the whole to live authentically, with vision and courage. The Grail represents the fulfillment of the highest spiritual potentialities of the human consciousness.

2. The Grail quest is the subject of chapters 10 and 11 of my book *Walking on Water*.

In Chrétien's Grail romance, Perceval finds two kings in the Grail Castle, the Grail King and the Fisher King. The Grail King, clearly a God image, he sees only briefly but describes as "the most beautiful person he ever beheld." Perceval never sees the Grail King again, but he cannot forget what he saw. In the outer chamber of the castle is the wounded king. His name is Anfortas, from an old French word meaning Infirmity or "without strength." The two kings are the two parts of the human soul, the godly part and the broken part. The godly king is the one that holds the castle together, that accepts the gospel, that always says "Yes" to God. The broken king is the part that feels obsessed, neurotic, and sick. Both parts are in us. The hero's task is not only to discover his True Self, but also to bring the two kings, the two parts, together.

As a young man, the Fisher King, like all adolescents, exhibits great potential, but he has not yet earned the position of King. He rides forth from his castle with the cry "Amor!," appropriate for youth, but not for the guardianship of the Grail. As he rides forth, a pagan knight emerges from the woods. The two level their lances at one another and attack. The lance of the Fisher King kills the pagan, but the pagan's lance castrates the Fisher King.

What this means is that religious and rationalistic dualism—highlighted by the Christian separation of matter and spirit, of secular and sacred life, of natural and supernatural grace—has castrated Western civilization. The European and American mind and life, as it were, have been emasculated by the separation. Vital spirituality, which results from the union of matter and spirit, has been killed. This, for me, is one of the insights of the nursery rhyme, "Humpty Dumpty sat on a wall, / Humpty Dumpty had a great fall. / All the king's horses / And all the king's men, / Couldn't put Humpty together again." While the original meaning may have alluded to the death of England's King Richard III, whose brutal reign ended in 1485, or to a large cannon that fell from a castle parapet and shattered, Humpty Dumpty is often drawn as an egg and interpreted as a symbolic reference to human or social fragility. Viewed spiritually, human brokenness can only be healed by integrating matter and spirit.

In the Grail romance, the pagan represents Nature, a person from the suburbs of Eden and thus an idealization of spirituality and union. On the head of his lance is written the word "Grail," which is to say, that nature intends the Grail, intends authenticity, integration, and wholeness. Spiritual life is not an add-on to life, not a supernatural virtue imposed upon it, but the flowering and fulfillment of human life. The sense of the Grail is that Nature intends the Grail; the impulses of nature are what give authenticity to life, not rules imposed from an alien supernatural authority. Nature and spirit yearn for one other, and the Grail legends long for the union once again of what has been divided. The Grail is a reminder of the original singularity from which all life emerged, and our job—the task of those on the Grail quest—is to take God's original "Let It Be" and find ways to participate in the evolutionary fallout of creation by living, thinking, and proclaiming that message in our own experience.

Entry 4: Asking the Right Question

The Grail quest symbolizes an authentic life that is lived imaginatively and uniquely, in terms of its own volition, a way of thinking and living that carries itself midway between the opposites of good and evil, light and dark, wounded and healed. When Perceval, naïve yet noble of heart, comes to the Grail Castle, he meets the Fisher King, who is brought in on a litter, wounded yet kept alive simply by the presence of the Grail.

The court fool had prophesied long before that the Fisher King would be healed when an innocent fool arrived in the court and asked a specific question. It may shock us that a fool should have to undertake such a crucial role. However, what the myth is telling us is that only the naïve part of our being will heal and cure our Fisher King wound. It also tells us why the Fisher King cannot heal himself, and why, when he goes fishing, his pain is eased though not cured. For people to be truly healed, they must allow something entirely different from themselves to enter their consciousness and change them. They cannot be healed if they remain in the old Fisher King mentality. That is why the young fool part of ourselves must enter our life if we are to be cured. We must look to a foolish, innocent, part of ourselves for our cure. Many legends put our cure in the hands of a fool or someone most unlikely to carry healing power. The inner fool—someone or something most unlikely to carry healing power—is the only one who can touch our Fisher King wound.

Perceval enters the Grail Castle and beholds the wounded King. His compassion moves him to ask, "What ails you?," but he fails to ask the question because he had been taught by mentors that a knight does not ask personal or unnecessary questions. So he follows the rules, and the adventure fails. It takes Perceval years of ordeals, setbacks, and embarrassments (his entire adolescence, it seems), before he returns to the castle and asks the question that heals the King and heals society. The question is an expression of compassion, not of legalism, political correctness, or religious propriety. Compassion is the natural opening of the human heart to another, but it is also the inner fool healing his own Fisher King wound.[3]

The wasteland results when the rules and boundaries of the first half of life keep us locked in immature adolescent patterns, preventing us from our authentic second half of life. We humans live in two worlds, not only ideologically, but also developmentally. We live in the external world, the socialized world given to us by others, and we live in our own inner world. Spirituality helps us achieve a harmonious relationship between these polarities. As members of society, we must learn to live by the rules of society. However, we cannot allow the external to control the internal. The internal world must be valued and nurtured as well, even if this impetus violates the expectations of others.

When we ponder the Grail quest, many dualities come to mind, including social, psychological, cosmological, philosophical, and religious. Those acquainted with the history of Christianity are aware that during its first five centuries, there were many Christianities, many ways of being Christian. Eventually, in the late fourth century, the only religion allowed in the Roman Empire was the Christian religion, wedded to the remnants of Roman imperialism in what became known as Christendom. The West's conversion to Christianity required the demise of paganism, and with it, the demise of nonduality as a way of thinking and living.

One of the interesting aspects of the Grail legends as we remember them is that they developed about five centuries after Christianity was imposed upon Europe. Properly understood, these legends represent a coming together of two traditions, Celtic pagan and non-Celtic Christian traditions, an amalgam not unlike the earlier Canaanite pagan and Israelite traditions, or the later Judeo-Christian and Greco-Roman synthesis.

Entry 5: Thin Places

The way back to the biblical Garden, to the underlying unity and harmony of the universe, requires us to become co-creators with God, to embody God's creative "Let It Be" program, thus becoming citizens of God's eternal

---

3. Perhaps this is what Jesus meant when he spoke the proverb, "Doctor, cure yourself!" (Luke 4:23).

kingdom. To return to the Garden, to become what Jesus called kingdom people or what Paul called co-heirs with Christ, we need to rediscover liminality, the creative, rejuvenating spirituality that lies both within and beyond time and space. Liminality often presents itself to us in times of silence, meditation, and rest, sometimes in the still of the night, but more often at twilight or dawn, in times and places that transcend locality and temporality, singularities known as "thin places." According to the biblical record, Jesus went to deserted places to pray, doing so regularly (see Matt 14:23; Luke 5:16; 6:12; 9:28; 22:39–46). As we discover, the times and places may change throughout our life. Liminality requires flexibility, even spontaneity. However, engaging with liminality is not about lacking focus or being lazy. This is holy work; at stake is our salvation.

"Thin places," a metaphor taken from Celtic spirituality, refers to places, objects, events, persons, and other phenomena that are understood as being transparent to the divine. The concept has its home in an understanding of reality that affirms at least two layers or dimensions of reality: (a) the visible world of ordinary experience and (b) the sacred, understood as the source of all things but also as a presence interpenetrating everything. In "thin places" the boundary between the two levels becomes diaphanous and permeable.[4]

As "places" of beauty, fascination, and intrigue, thin places stir the imagination; as "places" of honesty and courage, where truth and justice prevail, they call us to action and selfless service; as "places" of conviction, inspiration, and empowerment, they challenge us to transformation; as "places" of insight, wisdom, and discernment, they call us to spiritual renewal.

Thin places are paradoxical: they are places of power and weakness; they provide weal and woe, bliss and pain; they are found in crosses and cancers but also in resurrection and remission; they may be ordinary, or extraordinary; sometimes they delight us, other times they perplex us; they are places of wonder but also of terror. When they surround us, we are enraptured, and when they fade, we experience despair. Thin places fuel the imagination, foster risk-taking, feed the spirit, and foment human transformation. They have the ability to alter our way of thinking, transform our character, and renew our souls.

Thin places are liminal spaces—in-between spaces, windows, doorways, thresholds, intersections, portals, transitions—that usher us from one state or space to another. They signify boundaries, beginnings, and

4. Borg, *Meaning of Jesus*, 250.

becomings that open the way to something new, expanding our awareness and providing unity to our reality. For Christians they encompass activities, events, persons, objects, and experiences by which the Father speaks, in which Christ is present, and through which the breath of the Spirit blows freest. Thin places are transparent to the divine because God is there: through-and-around-and-over-and-under-and-behind-and-before-and-within them.

C. S. Lewis, one of the twentieth century's foremost Christian authors, knew about "thin places." He wrote about them in the *Chronicles of Narnia*, a set of seven children's classics in which he created a land of wonder and enchantment called Narnia. Following this publication, Lewis rigorously defended the fairy tale against those who claimed that it gives a false conception of life. The fairy tale, he argued, like the myth, arouses longing for more ideal worlds but at the same time gives the real world a new depth. While Lewis's Narnia *Chronicles* remind us of other works, such as the Alice-in-Wonderland-like opening of *The Lion, the Witch and the Wardrobe* or the voyage made by the *Dawn Treader*, which is akin to the voyage of Odysseus, Lewis blends Christian themes with events created from the rich world of fantasy. A dominant idea in his stories is that of an earlier time when reality was more harmonious and unified. It was Lewis's hope that upon reading these stories, children (and adults) would return to the "real world" with a new perspective, their minds opened to the possibilities of an unseen spiritual world and to the limits of merely human intellect and undeveloped imagination.

Lewis was referring to "thin places" without using the term. He knew, as children of all ages discover when they read his Narnia *Chronicles* or J. K. Rowling's Harry Potter books, that our world is alive with liminalities (threshold spaces between the sacred and the mundane); pictures, closets, fireplaces, train stations—any object, event, or person can open our minds to the possibilities and transport us to an unseen spiritual world.

While we are intrigued by the proverb, "Physician, heal thyself," what does it mean? How can we heal ourselves? The answer, at least in part, is this; we need to find sacred time and sacred place, meaning, we need to discover liminality. While liminality can best be experienced in silence and times of rest such as daydreaming, gazing, pondering, meditating, worshipping, singing, and individual and small-group Bible study, it can also be experienced in creative arts such as music, painting, and writing, and through activities such as yoga, tai chi, gardening, swimming, kayaking, cross-country skiing, hiking, running, cycling, and numerous other rhythmic and aerobic activities that ground and connect us with the larger whole. Anything therapeutic is holistic, for what is good for the body is good for the mind, and what is healthy for the body and mind connects us to the soul and spirit within. Such interaction, even in its initial stages, enhances spirituality, for spirituality is at work in all holistic endeavors.

Personality and Spirituality

Entry 1: Temperament and Personality

People are naturally different from one another in fundamental ways: they want different things, have different aims, think and learn differently, and believe differently. And of course, how they act and emote is governed by individual needs, desires, and beliefs. In many cases, differences in others trigger negative responses in others. Seeing others differing from us, it is easy to conclude that when they differ from us in behavior or response, it is due to some malady or flaw. Our job, at least for those near us, might seem to be to correct their flaws, making those near us more like us. Such a task, however, is doomed from the start. Our attempts to change others, whether spouse, sibling, lover, co-worker or friend, can produce change, but the result is likely more a distortion than a transformation. Besides, trying to change others is futile and counterproductive, in that most of the differences between human beings are essentially good.

The belief that people are fundamentally alike appears to be a twentieth century notion. The idea is probably related to the growth of democracy in the Western world. If we are equals, we must be alike. Classical psychologists such as Freud, Adler, Sullivan, Fromm, and their followers affirmed the idea of singular motivation. Whatever the drive, whether motivated by Eros, power, social solidarity, or the search after Self, each personality school made one instinct primary for everybody.

Swiss psychiatrist Carl Jung disagreed. He noted that people differ in fundamental ways, even though they all possess the same instincts to drive them from within. No instinct is more important than another; what is most significant for most individuals, however, is their preference for how they function. Because people are characterized by their preference for given functions, they may be "typed" by their preference.

The developments of psychology in the twentieth century were amazing. Behaviorists, cognitivists, constructivists and others studied the nature of human beings. Most of these theories tried to answer the question whether human personality is determined by nature (i.e. heredity) or nurture (i.e. environment or learning). Theories that claimed human personality is a function of nature (or heredity) are called temperament theories. Temperament is that aspect of our personalities that is genetically based and therefore innate. That does not mean that a temperament theory rules out the role of environment; rather, a temperament theory does not focus on environment. It should also be noted that the issue of temperament is much older than psychology itself. It has a history of at least five thousand years.

Entry 2: Myers-Briggs Type Inventory, Part I

One of the most important contributions of Carl Jung to modern psychological thought is his theory of personality types. While Jung's monumental study, *Psychological Types*, requires a good deal of psychological and philosophical background to be understood, the essentials of his theory have been elaborated and developed by others, including the personality type indicator developed by Isabel Briggs-Myers and her mother Katherine Cook Briggs known as the Myers-Briggs Type Indicator (MBTI), which charts sixteen possible personality types in terms of Jungian type theory. Today, thanks to this sorting device, many Jungian concepts are widely known and accepted and millions have taken the MBTI, which is widely applied in team building, organization development, business management, education, and career and marriage counseling. Understanding one's type is making a welcome change in people's lives globally, in a wide diversity of situations.

The MBTI, now available online, is not really a test, but a sorter of preferences on four scales or categories, each consisting of two opposite poles. At the conclusion of the test you receive four letters, which comprise your personality type. They indicate the differences in people that result from

- where they prefer to focus their attention
  (Extraversion or Introversion)—E or I;

- the way they prefer to take in information
  (Sensing or Intuition)—S or N;

- the way they prefer to make decisions
  (Thinking or Feeling)—T or F;

- how they orient themselves to the external world
  (Judging or Perceiving)—J or P.

These preferences produce sixteen different kinds of people, interested in different things and drawn to different fields. Each type has its own inherent strengths as well as its likely blind spots. However, these types often blend into one another, inasmuch as each of us is a unique combination of these attitudes and functions. Discovering one's personality type is extremely beneficial, for it influences career choices, marriage choices, learning style, spiritual journeys, theological understanding, and much more. Learning one's personality type also makes us more aware and sensitive to the psychological needs, preferences, and differences of those around us.

Entry 3: Myers-Briggs Type Inventory, Part II

If we are to care for, work with, or love other people, we need to know what makes them unique, and we will need to help them develop their own type potential and relate to them in ways that are meaningful to them. For example, people with developed sensate functions are usually characterized by simplicity in life style. They are interested in concrete facts and seldom in fantasy or make-believe. The basic interest of the intuitive type is in acquiring wisdom. Unlike sensors, they are fascinated by fantasy, hunches, and imaginative possibilities. However, routine tasks often bore them and they often do not follow through. They need new challenges, new problems, variety, and change. The thinking type wants things understandable and in logical order; consequently, thinkers do not like exceptions to rules. Often they make good executives, because the good of the whole takes precedence over individual desires. They can make decisions, but sometimes their apparent coldness alienates other types. The feeling type is most often characterized by an ability to experience joy. It is important to realize that the word "feeling" does not mean emotion, but rather signifies the capacity to evaluate data according to human values. Feelers are interested in other human beings and what influences them. They are excellent at getting along with others and are often found in the helping professions. Making unpleasant decisions affecting the lives of others is difficult for them.

Of the two middle letters in one's type (S or N, T or F), one will be the dominant function, the home base of operations, and the other will be the auxiliary, one's second most important function. It is impossible to love others unless we can recognize their type and place an adequate value upon their primary function. But here's a caveat: We should never try to have other persons change their type. They will do best if they develop what they are by nature.

When people are young, their energy is directed toward development of their most preferred, dominant function, and their behavior reflects this. For example, an introverted Feeling child will be a quiet observer, with an instinctive sense of others' feelings; an introverted Intuitive child will be actively exploring the variety of the surrounding world. An extraverted Thinking child will try to order his environment to fit with his logical principles; an introverted Thinking child will try to internally make sense of her world. Once children develop skills in their dominant function, the focus of energy and attention then shifts to the auxiliary function. The primary task of type development in the first part of life is to establish the leadership provided by the dominant function, balanced by the healthy development of the auxiliary function. Later in life, the focus of development shifts, this time to the less-preferred functions, aspects of the individual's personality and potential that have only minimally been explored. This redirection of energy is part of the midlife transition, which Jung saw as the gateway to later life development and satisfaction. The task of the second half of life, then, is to move toward full development of all of oneself, including those parts that were previously neglected and unrealized.

When people first learn Jung's theory, they often think the ideal is to develop all four functions with equal facility to achieve balance. That, however, is not how development works, for if a person tries to develop opposite ways of perceiving equally, for example, then neither Sensing nor Intuition will receive the focus or attention necessary to become fully reliable. The four functions tend to pull in opposite directions: Sensing, to the reality of the present; Intuition, to the possibility of the future; Thinking, to decisions based on objective logic; and Feeling, to decisions based on subjective values. People who do not establish dominance of each pair of functions are inconsistent in their behavior, pulled first in one direction and then another. The goal of type development, then, is not equal development and use of all the functions, but rather the ability to use each mental process with some facility when it is appropriate.

In conclusion, Jung's model of the human journey is based on the following assumptions:

- each person has an innate urge to grow

- the human psyche is self-regulating and capable of healing itself

- development means developing conscious control over and facility in the use of a function

- development is an interaction between a person's innate type preferences and the environment. If the environment is supportive, growth tends to follow innate type. If the environment is not supportive, the pattern may be affected by a person's adaptation to the requirements of the environment

- in the first half of life, growth takes the form of development of the preferred functions; in the second half of life, a person's focus of energy and attention naturally shifts to the less-preferred functions. This is a process of moving toward one's unexplored potential.

The following quote, noted in topic 3, summarizes Jung's understanding of the psychological-spiritual task during the second half of life: "Among all my patients in the second half of life—that is to say, over thirty-five—there has not been one whose problem in the last resort was not that of finding a religious outlook on life."

Entry 4: Holmes's Typology of Spirituality

Spirituality and personality are deeply interrelated, so much that neither function adequately apart from the other. As I state in *Dark Splendor*, my 2015 volume on spiritual fitness for the second half of life,

> Like cyclists on a tandem, personality and spirituality travel together through the journey of life. Riding in tandem, they are deeply influenced by conditions both internal (goals, moods, desires) and external to the self. When one leans, the other leans; where one starts, the other starts; if one stops, the other stops. Though not identical, they strive to be in sync, balancing one another in profound and intimate ways. Personality takes the lead, and where personality goes, spirituality follows, though not

blindly or passively. Spirituality has its own voice, and when its desires are addressed and heeded, personality thrives. When the two disagree, they must communicate, or the consequences can be disastrous. Cooperation always enhances the ride.[1]

Aware that spirituality is shaped by personality and unique to each individual, but also that "birds of a feather flock together," Urban Holmes[2] presents a helpful typology for the spiritual life revolving around four ways that people seek to understand the experience of God and its meaning for our times:

- Type I: sacramental (an intellectual, "thinking" spirituality)

- Type II: charismatic (a heartfelt, intuitive spirituality)

- Type III: mystical (a contemplative, introspective spirituality)

- Type IV: apostolic (an active, visionary spirituality)

Holmes calls his model the "Circle of Sensibility," and in it he delineates four styles of prayer, later configured as schools of spirituality. By "sensibility" he refers to the possibilities within individuals and communities as they seek to understand the experience of God and its meaning for our times. Holmes proposes the use of two intersecting lines placed within a circle. The vertical line creates a north-south axis, with Sensibility (Mind or Intellect) at the north pole and Affective (Heart or Emotion) at the south pole. The horizontal line creates an east-west axis, with Kataphatic (God as Revealed: known through images) at the east pole and Apophatic (God as Mystery: known mystically). His circle, divided into four quadrants, contains four schools of spirituality, which he labeled "speculative-kataphatic" (Type I spirituality), affective-kataphatic (Type II spirituality), affective-apophatic (Type III spirituality), and speculative-apophatic (Type IV spirituality).

Holmes's typology overlaps significantly with Jung's typology, as incorporated in the MBTI. Type I spirituality, an intellectual "thinking" spirituality, has been identified as "sacramental." Its primary aim is to aid persons in fulfilling their vocation in the world. This spirituality favors what it can see, touch, and vividly imagine. Type II spirituality, a sensate, heartfelt approach to spirituality, has been identified as "charismatic." Its primary aim is to achieve holiness of life through personal renewal. Type

1. Vande Kappelle, *Dark Splendor*, 23.
2. Holmes, *History of Christian Spirituality.*

III spirituality, which emphasizes being and direct experience of God, has been identified as "mystical." Its primary aim is union with the Holy, an unattainable goal, a journey that nevertheless continually impels the disciple onward. Type IV spirituality, a visionary, almost crusading type of spirituality, has been identified as "apostolic." Its primary aim is to obey God's will completely. Its major concerns are witness to God's reign and striving for justice and peace.

Entry 5: The Enneagram

The Enneagram represents an approach to personality that concerns itself with normal and high-functioning behavior, and it condenses a great deal of psychological insight into a compact system that is relatively easy to understand. The term "Enneagram" was introduced by George Gurdjieff (1879–1949), an eccentric Russian who traveled widely, particularly to Mount Athos, a rugged and isolated peninsula in Greece that is home to twenty Orthodox monasteries. There he learned esoteric practices helpful in opening human consciousness. He taught these practices to his study groups in St. Petersburg and Moscow in 1916. Gurdjieff called his system of principles of inner growth The Fourth Way, claiming it transcended the three traditional spiritual paths of the monk, the yogi, and the fakir. He taught that it is possible to live The Fourth Way while active in the world, rather than detached from life in an isolated community of like-minded seekers.

The word Enneagram stems from the Greek *ennea*, meaning "nine," and *grammos*, meaning "points." The Enneagram refers to "a nine-pointed star diagram that can be used to map the process of any event from its inception through all the stages of that event's progress in the material world."[3] The Enneagram's value is in its ease of use, rooted in a time-tested tradition of understanding human nature—how it is formed, broken, and healed. The Enneagram types persons into one of nine boxes (the Perfectionist/Reformer, the Helper/Giver, the Achiever/Performer, the Idealist/Tragic Romantic, the Investigator/Observer, the Loyalist/Critic, the Enthusiast/Epicure, the Protector/Boss, and the Peacemaker/Mediator), providing information about the way that individuals are likely to behave and therefore to get along. While lessening the tension of having to live with the mystery of the unknown, the Enneagram is not a fixed system. It is a model of interconnecting lines that indicate a dynamic movement, in which each of

3. Palmer, *The Enneagram*, 10.

us has the potentials of all nine types, or points, although we identify most strongly with the issues of our own type. Interconnecting lines indicate the versatility of movement available to the individual, as well as specific relationships between the different types of individuals.

Underlying the Enneagram is a distinction between one's essential nature and one's acquired personality. Essential nature is described as "hard wired" or what is "one's own," the potential with which we were born, rather than the personality we have acquired through education, the influence of authority figures, beliefs, and personal ideas. The Enneagram's nine-pointed star suggests that there are nine major aspects of essential being and that each may be approached in different ways. The search for a particular aspect of essence is motivated by the suffering caused by its absence. For example, if you are chronically afraid, then you have suffered the loss of the child's essential trust, whether in the environment or in others. Therefore searching for courage becomes a motive in your life.

The realization that we are acting contrary to our essential nature indicates the presence of an inner observer. The Enneagram system encourages the practice of self-observation, whereby individuals focus their attention inwardly in order to recognize habitual patterns within their minds. The fact that one can observe and talk about one's own habits of thinking and feeling from the point of view of a detached observer helps to make these habits less compulsive and automatic.

In her book on the Enneagram, Helen Palmer identifies nine chief features (passions) of the emotional life (anger, pride, deceit, envy, greed, fear, gluttony, lust, and sloth). These emotional patterns are part of one's emotional shadow or the acquired personality, stemming from the need to cope with early family life. If a child develops in a healthy manner, then the passions are akin to mere tendencies, which can be identified with relative ease and dealt with accordingly. But if the psychological situation is severe, then one of the shadow issues becomes an obsessional preoccupation. In this case the capacity for self-observation weakens and the individual cannot move on to other things. The hope is that by identifying one's own Chief Feature, one can observe the many ways in which this habit has gained control over one's life. In this case, one's Chief Feature (one's passion), a neurotic habit that developed during childhood, can also become a personal mentor.

Addictive Patterns and Behavior: The Problem

Entry 1: The Nature of Addiction

WE CLOSE OUR DISCUSSION of the inward journey with three topics central to spiritual health and well-being: awareness of addiction in our lives; overcoming ever-present addictive patterns of behavior; and achieving a healthy, holistic lifestyle.

Addiction is a modern-day epidemic. More than 500 people die every hour as a result of an addiction related disorder or an overdose, and addiction is estimated to cost the United States more than 600 billion dollars every year in health-care costs, lost productivity, and crime. As a result, families are destroyed, careers are lost, and lives are wasted. Moreover, the problem is only getting worse. Indeed, today, more people than ever before see themselves as addicted or recovering from addictive or compulsive behavior. In a national survey conducted in 2012, one in ten American adults—more than twenty-three million people—said they had kicked some type of drug or alcohol addiction in their lifetime. Added to this number, at least another twenty-three million adults currently suffer from some type of substance use disorder.[1] That doesn't include the millions who consider themselves addicted to or recovering from behaviors like sex, gambling, or online activities, not does it include food-related disorders or compulsive consumerism.

What is addiction, and how do we know if we are addicted? Speaking sociologically, we are addicted because we live in addictive societies that turn us into consumers and materialists. Speaking biologically, we are addicted because that is how we are hard wired. Speaking spiritually, we are addicted

1. Szalavitz, *Unbroken Brain*, 2.

because we seek spiritual satisfaction through things other than God. Humans can be addicted to most any object, ideology, and belief, but they cannot be addicted to the true God, for reasons disclosed later on.

Addiction, as you might have guessed, is not limited to substances. Humans regularly become obsessed with work, performance, hygiene, responsibility, intimacy, vanity, and personal appearance, as well as to being liked, helping others, and an almost endless list of other behaviors. Viewed naturally, as patterns related to vocation, parenting, maturity, and other social skills, such behaviors are not only normal but also necessary and even virtuous. In most cases, the absence of such factors can be alarming, for this deficiency can result in depression, withdrawal, boredom, indolence, and even in more dangerous and antisocial behavior such as violence and crime. However, when concerns with performance, appearance, and responsibility become compulsive, tolerance and withdrawal are clearly evident. In such cases, no matter how much achievement, approval, or intimacy one experiences, it is never enough.

How we conceptualize or view addiction affects not only our understanding of its nature but also our approach to recovery. Addiction is not a sin or a disease, as many commonly suppose. Broadly understood, addiction is a universal condition that plagues not only humans but also all animal species. Viewed as compulsive behavior that traps people in patterns of repressive behavior, addiction may be said to characterize every human being. This seems particularly obvious when the topic is examined morally, from the traditional sin-salvation paradigm. Observed morally, addictive behavior is labeled sinful, for all behavior that is self-serving and compulsive is considered defective and therefore immoral. Such characterization, however, is unhelpful and, I believe, ultimately unchristian. If humans sin, does that make them sinners? If you answer "yes," what happens when you examine the question from a less theological perspective? For example, if someone acts obsessively or compulsively in a given situation, does that automatically mean they have an obsessive-compulsive disorder (OCD)? Furthermore, if a person kills someone unintentionally in an auto accident, is that person a murderer? Surely the answer to such questions is "no."

To think simplistically about addiction, labeling everyone a sinner or an addict, is misguided. If all people are sinners because all sin, are all people equally saints when they perform good deeds or act compassionately? Processes responsible for addiction to alcohol and narcotics are related to commitment to ideas, work, relationships, power, moods, fantasies, and an endless variety of other things. For those inclined to think ethically or moralistically about human behavior, it might be more useful to introduce a third category, to characterize the majority of human beings as neither sinners nor saints but rather as survivors.

When examining topics as emotional and subjective as addiction, it is also common *to think stereotypically*: others are addicts, we are not; others are morally defective, we are not; others are wrong, we are right; others are lazy, unproductive, violent, promiscuous, immature, unreliable, and deceptive, whereas we are industrious, productive, calm, loyal, mature, reliable, and truthful. Ultimately, dualistic thinking and "us" versus "them" attitudes are unhelpful. Twisted stereotypes have long been used to demonize and dehumanize people of other races, classes, creeds, and nationalities, to discriminate against those different from ourselves.

Essay 2: Pathways to Addiction, Part I

By itself, nothing is addictive. Technically speaking, addiction manifests itself only in certain contexts. When a combination of factors in a person's social and cultural development—biological, psychological, social, and cultural—align to produce harmful and even destructive behavior that is difficult to stop, addiction is a potential consequence.

Contrary to popular belief, addiction is not solely a choice or a craving, though both are involved, and it isn't simply taking drugs or getting stuck in destructive patterns. Nor is addiction a chronic, progressive brain disease like Alzheimer's. Rather, *speaking technically*, addiction is a learning disorder, a pattern of learned behavior.

Though the idea that learning is central to addiction is not universally acknowledged, it is becoming widely accepted by clinicians and theoreticians alike, going back to the pioneering efforts of Alfred Lindesmith's 1947 text, *Opiate Addiction*.[2] Since then, countless authors and researchers have made critical contributions to the learning model of addiction. To stress that addiction is a learning disorder does not mean that biology is not involved, nor does this view imply that medical treatment, including medication, is not often useful and sometimes essential. However, when the role of learning is ignored, addiction is then forced into a category of medical illness or moral failure, where it does not always fit or necessarily belong.

2. This earlier work was revised and published in 1968 as *Addiction and Opiates*.

Traditionally, developmental disorders that appeared in early childhood, even when extreme, tended to be dismissed as phases or simple misbehavior. Now, however, stimulant medication is being prescribed to more than 6 percent of schoolchildren, by contrast with the 1960s, when it was used by less than a fraction of a single percent. How can we account for such a drastic change in perspective? The answer is that now virtually all psychiatric disorders—including schizophrenia, bipolar disorder, and personality disorders—as well as addiction, have been found to be profoundly shaped by learning during development. As we are now aware, almost every disorder that affects mental function in childhood and adolescence has a learned component. Since brain development cannot progress properly without experience, knowing how learning molds the brain over time is crucial to our understanding of addiction.

When we understand the importance of learning and development in addiction, many of its contradictions are resolved and it becomes easier to see why addiction is neither a moral failing nor a brain disease in the traditional sense. That's because learning produces change in the brain, based on a person's experience. This makes each brain—and each addiction—unique.

According to Maia Szalavitz, perhaps America's most influential journalist covering addiction and drugs, learning or developmental disorders display four distinguishing features:[3]

1. They start early in life. Since most brain development depends on experience, environmental influences in childhood (ranging from parental and peer influence to chemical exposures) can determine whether wiring differences in the brain become disorders, disabilities, advantages, or some mix of all three.

2. They are frequently associated with high intelligence. While developmental disorders such as Down syndrome may be accompanied by reduced intelligence, this is not the case with autism, dyslexia, ADHD, addictive disorders, or related mental illnesses. Many of these conditions are actually accompanied by high IQ.

3. They are greatly impacted by timing. Because healthy development unfolds in precise patterns, the sequencing of environmental influences, particularly social ones, is critically important. Missing an experience at one stage of development may be trivial, but it can derail learning at another stage. Indeed, at certain stages of development,

3. Szalavitz, *Unbroken Brain*, 43–45.

notably during infancy and adolescence, the brain expects particular experiences, and if these are not delivered at the right time and in the right order, development can be skewed. If important input at one of these stages is missed, it is difficult for someone to catch up later.

4. Their progression can be changed by well-timed intervention. For example, infancy is vital to language development. Before infant screening for deafness became widespread, early hearing loss was commonly misdiagnosed as intellectual disability. Because deaf children did not learn language when their brains were most receptive to it, they appeared to have difficulty with grammar and other skills. Similarly, early intervention can significantly reduce many problems related to developmental disorders such as autism and ADHD (attention deficit hyperactivity disorder). The same may be true for early intervention for addictive behaviors.

As developmental disorders, that is, as problems involving timing and learning, addictive patterns can be outgrown in a surprisingly large number of cases, particularly when they involve repeated choices. Additional factors, including early-life trauma such as sexual abuse, parental violence, neglect, bullying, and other forms of rejection, also play an important role in addiction. As commonly assumed, addiction doesn't happen to people simply because they are exposed to a drug and begin taking it regularly. Nor is it the inevitable outcome of a certain personality type or genetic background, though these factors play a role. Rather, it is a learned relationship between the timing and pattern of the exposure to substances or other potentially addictive experiences and a person's predispositions, cultural and physical environment, and social and emotional needs. Because it is a learning behavior, it has a history rooted in a person's individual, social, and cultural development. Addiction, then, is a coping style that becomes maladaptive when the behavior persists despite ongoing negative consequences.

A common and generally misleading approach to addiction is the search for a single incident—a Rosebud moment—that explains everything. Like the word "Rosebud" in the movie *Citizen Kane*, there may be cases where this is true, and as research suggests, discerning such a moment or creating a coherent narrative out of one's experience may help recovery from trauma, which is extremely common in chemical addiction. However, as with many developmental disorders, there are often various influences and rarely a single cause. Likewise, there are many turning points in which one's developmental trajectory can change entirely. Most stories of addiction involve at least some if not all of the following features:

- temperamental susceptibility to addiction

- genetic factors suspected to increase risk of psychiatric disorders

- neglect by family

- rejection by peers

- social inadequacy, loneliness, and low self-esteem

- anger and rebellion

- peer pressure and the effects of one's cultural setting (whether permissive, dismissive, individualistic, narcissistic, et cetera)

- seeking glamour, participating in the "good life"

- needing to feel good, to increase pleasure and self-worth

- experiencing trauma, either one's own or in one's ancestral history

- needing to fit in, to feel "cool," sophisticated, mature, and strong

- partaking for "effect"; seeking to recreate the "first experience," the first "high," the first love, the first sense of power or control, et cetera.

Entry 3: Addiction and the Brain

Substance abuse is just one of many ways that people learn to cope. And since coping behavior is essential to psychological survival, coping methods learned during childhood and adolescence become deeply engrained in the brain. Hence, brain maturation is an important factor. As a developmental disorder, addiction is more likely to appear in some stages of life than in others. In addiction, adolescence is the highest risk period because this is when the brain changes to prepare for adult sexuality and responsibilities and when people begin to develop ways of coping that will serve them for the rest of their lives.

Speaking biologically, we are all addicted; to be alive is to be addicted. That's how we are hard wired. We all struggle with addiction, and to function without customary items leads not only to a craving for them, but also to anxiety and even physical discomfort. As I argue in my 2019 book

Addiction, addiction is a pattern of learned behavior that utilizes ancient mental pathways designed to promote survival and reproduction. Since those are the fundamental tasks of all biological organisms, brain patterns produce highly motivated behavior. When neural connections intended to promote eating, reproduction, parenting, and social relationships are diverted into addiction, their blessings can become curses.

Like other parts of the body, the human brain is composed of cells. There are various kinds of cells in the brain, but the most significant are nerve cells or neurons. Each neuron is a living being, for it has its own unique life and experience. Yet each neuron responds to the activities of cells and substances in its environment. Neurons both initiate and respond to a wide variety of electrical and chemical stimuli. While the brain has a limited capacity for regeneration, meaning that neural pathways in the brain can be created throughout the life of an individual, even during one's old age, the vast majority of neurons in the brain are formed by the time of birth.

The brain may be viewed as a "colony" in which billions of these tiny cells live. Some groups (local groups) of neurons are located close together in the same areas of the brain and may or may not work together. Other groups (functional systems) are made up of cells that do work together to accomplish certain tasks; they may be located close together or at some distance from one another. For example, the cells involved in thinking may be located quite near one another in the frontal lobe. A similar group of cells near the inside center of the brain affects body temperature, while a group nearer the spinal cord governs the level of wakefulness and attentiveness. However, most functional systems involve the collaboration of cells that are widely separated within the brain. They connect with one another through a long fiber or axon.

Nerve cells send messages through connections called synapses. An average neuron has twenty thousand connections with other cells, and some as many as two hundred thousand. At each synapse, communication takes place when the axon of one cell releases a chemical called a *neurotransmitter*. This chemical passes across the tiny synapse between the cells and is received by a chemical structure called a *neuroreceptor* on the next cell. In addition to responding to neurotransmitters from other cells, neuroreceptors are also sensitive to chemicals such as hormones, which are produced elsewhere in the body and circulate through the bloodstream. Foreign chemicals such as caffeine, nicotine, narcotics, and other drugs also reach neuroreceptors through the bloodstream and can exert powerful influences on the neurons.[4]

Through an important mechanism called feedback, cells often respond to the messages they receive by affecting the cells that sent the message originally. Feedback not only changes the messages being communicated, but it also helps maintain important balances in the body. The messages carried by specific neurotransmitters may stimulate, inhibit, or facilitate a cell's activity. This vast array of interactions, in turn, give rise to human experience and behavior. All thoughts and feelings, all sensations and memories, are mediated by the transmission of electrochemical energies along the bodies and fibers of nerve cells and across synapses. Each mental function is determined by which nerve cells and synapses are active, in what sequence, and by what neurotransmitter chemicals are released and received.

In order to appreciate how the brain functions, we need to emphasize the importance of balance and equilibrium in brain activity. All brain functioning, like the rest of bodily activity, depends upon delicate shifts of balance among chemicals, cells, and systems of cells. The interconnectivity of nerve cells is so extensive that anything happening anywhere within the nervous system produces effects elsewhere. A change in one cell shifts the balance of its local group and of all its functional systems. These changes, in turn, affect the larger systems of the brain, and these then cause changes in the other systems of the body. Knowing something of the complexity of the brain, of how brain cells work, and the necessity of maintaining natural balances, is essential to understanding how the brain becomes addicted.

Sadly, the brain never completely forgets what it has learned. Years after a major addiction has been conquered, the smallest association, the tiniest taste, can fire up old cellular patterns once again. From the standpoint of psychology, this means we can never become so well adjusted that we can stop being vigilant. From a neurological viewpoint, it means the cells of our recovery systems can never eradicate the countless other systems that have been addicted. From a spiritual perspective, it means that no matter how much grace we receive, we remain forever dependent upon its continuing flow.

4. May, *Addiction and Grace*, 68–69.

Entry 4: Addiction and Love

People looking for love, whether due to neglect or abandonment by parents, or as the result of failure or rejection in relationships, are at risk of addiction. Surprisingly, people obsessed and driven about relationships, as well as those seeking extreme experience, are also at risk. Since addiction was first described or diagnosed, it has been compared to love. Before compulsive drug use was seen as a disease, it was associated with excessive love. Such correlation was often made by poets and songwriters, who regularly linked sexual passion with desire for particular substances. However, it was not until 1975, when Stanton Peele and Archie Brodsky published *Love and Addiction*, that these passions received a thorough comparative examination. Through meticulous evaluation, the authors illustrated how unhealthy relationships—whether with drugs or with people—share fundamental qualities.

For example, nearly every behavior seen in addiction is found in romantic love. Obsession with the qualities and particulars of the beloved may be compared with the craving addicted individuals experience if the object of their addiction is unavailable. In some cases, people engage in extreme, uncharacteristic, or even immoral behavior to ensure access. In such cases, withdrawal prompts anxiety and feat; only the drug or loved one can relieve this suffering. Both conditions profoundly alter people's priorities and behavior.

Like addiction, misguided love is a problem of learning. In love, people learn powerful associations between their lovers and nearly everything about them and around them. In addiction, these connections are made with the drug or the compulsive behavior. As visits to certain locations or hearing a specific song can trigger thoughts of a loved one, so certain experiences and memories can spur longing for alcohol or drugs.

We now know that we are fundamentally interdependent—psychologically and physically. Babies, for example, need to be held and cuddled for their stress system to be properly regulated. Without repeated, loving care by the same few people, infants are at high risk for lifelong psychiatric and behavioral problems. During the 1930s and '40s, before this was widely known, one in three infants raised by rotating staff in orphanages died—essentially from lack of individualized love. Their physical needs had been met, but not their emotional ones.

While romantic relationships are not necessary for health, having at least some close relationships is. Research indicates that loneliness can be as dangerous to health as smoking, and more harmful than obesity. In fact, the more and higher-quality relationships a person has, the more mentally and physically healthy they tend to be. Improving relational health improves health in general, for children as well as adults.

Addicted people and those in recovery need loving, positive, relationships. When these are missing, obsessive craving will lead them into unhealthy relationships. Genuine love is the highest and best experience of humanity, and the presence of caring people in the lives of addicted individuals not only help meet unmet needs, but also help them distinguish between good and bad relationships. Love is real when it expands and enhances one's life, and troubling and problematic when it contracts or impairs life. The following rule is helpful: *If your love of a person, interest, or behavior spurs creativity, connection, and kindness, it is not an addiction; if a pattern, attitude, or relationship makes you isolated, dull, and mean, it is an addiction.*[5]

Entry 5: Addiction and Attachment

As we conclude our examination of the causes of addiction—associated with traumatic experiences at home, school, and society as well as with personality traits and disorders due to genetics and nurture—we need to consider another source of addiction, America's attachment to wealth and material possessions. Because many of us have more than we need, we should be happy and satisfied. Instead, we seek more, and as a result suffer stress, discontent, and insecurity. The reason is clear: material desires, while not necessarily bad, have a tendency to become addictive because instead of making us whole, they remind us how incomplete, needy, and empty we are.

In the past several centuries, the human community has divided into two distinct worlds: a "first" world filled with opulence, luxury, and material excess, and a "third" world characterized by deprivation, poverty, and struggle. Whereas first and third worlds could formerly be distinguished along national boundaries, increasingly one finds pockets of wealth surrounded by ever widening regions of impoverishment. Most of the world's population is now growing up in winner-take-all economies, where the main goal of individuals is to get whatever they can for

5. Szalavitz, *Unbroken Brain*, 152.

themselves. Within this economic landscape, selfishness and materialism are being seen as goals of life.[6]

This global reality exists, however, only because each one of us readily converted to the ideology of consumerism and materialism. Indeed, mass conversion seems already to have occurred. Vast numbers of us are coming to accept the idea that to be well, we first have to be well off. And many of us, unfortunately, are learning to evaluate our identity in terms of our own well-being and accomplishment, not by looking inward at our spirit or integrity, but by looking outward at what we have and what we can buy. Similarly, we have adopted a worldview in which the worth and success of others is judged not by their apparent wisdom, kindness, or community contributions, but in terms of whether they possess the right clothes, the right car, and more generally, the right "stuff."

Perhaps the most insidious aspect of this modern measure of worth is that it is not simply about having enough, but about having more than others do. That is, feelings of personal worth are based on how one's financial resources and possessions compares with that of others. Accordingly, at all levels of wealth one can find individuals who crave gadgets that are ever more expensive, status symbols, and image builders, and who subjectively feel that they need more than they currently have. As advertising executives have known for decades, people become good consumers only when they convert mere "desires" into urgent "needs." By this criterion, most of us have become good consumers.

What does research show? Does money buy happiness? Does affluence make us healthier and better adjusted psychologically? What happens to the quality of our lives when we value materialism? It would be one thing if the promises of the consumer society were real, but they are not. The formidable body of research into consumerism indicates a surprising and quite counter-intuitive fact, that even when people obtain more money and material goods, they do not become more satisfied with their lives, or more psychologically healthy as a result. More specifically, once people are above the poverty levels of income, gains in wealth have little to no payoff in terms of happiness or well-being. In addition, according to the research results that Tim Kasser reports in his 2002 *The High Price of Materialism*, merely aspiring to have greater wealth or more material possessions is likely to be associated with increased personal unhappiness. The American dream, it

6. Richard Ryan's "Foreword" to Kasser, *High Price of Materialism*, ix.

seems, has a dark side, and the pursuit of wealth and possessions might actually be undermining our well-being.[7]

As Kasser shows, people with strong materialistic values and desires report more symptoms of anxiety, are at greater risk for depression, low self-esteem, and problems of intimacy, and experience more frequent physical discomfort than those who are less materialistic. They watch more television, use more alcohol and drugs, and have more impoverished personal relationships. Even in sleep, their dreams seem to be infected with anxiety and distress. And these results are the same for all individuals, regardless of age, income, or culture.

7. Kasser, *High Price of Materialism*, 9.

Addictive Patterns and Behavior: The Solution

Entry 1: Awareness and Addiction

When we humans are faced with a task, we can respond in one of three ways: we can avoid the experience, we can be overwhelmed by it, or we can confront it. While each response can produce addictive behavior, depending on temperament and experience, the third is the best candidate, at least for most human beings. Having addressed the nature of addiction and its causes, this topic examines the solution to addiction, what we call "awareness," by which we mean self-awareness and self-control, something addicted individuals essentially relinquish.

For generations psychologist thought that virtually all self-defeating behavior was caused by repression. However, addiction is a separate and even more self-defeating force, for it abuses freedom and makes us do things we really do not want to do. While repression stifles desire, addiction attaches desire, bonding and enslaving the energy of desire to certain behaviors, things, or people. These objects of attachment then become preoccupations and obsessions; they come to rule our lives. In this light, we can see why traditional psychotherapy, which is based on the release of repression, has proven ineffective with addictions. It also shows why addiction is the most powerful psychic enemy of humanity's desire for God.

Addiction exists wherever human beings are internally compelled to give energy and priority to things that are not their ultimate desire. A state of compulsion, obsession, or preoccupation that enslaves our will and desire, addiction sidetracks and eclipses the energy of our deepest, truest desire for love and goodness. We succumb because the energy of our desire becomes attached to specific behaviors, objects, or people. Attachment, then, is the process that enslaves desire and creates the state of addiction.

In this sense, we are all addicted. Moreover, our addictions are our own worst enemies. They enslave us with chains that are of our own making and yet that, paradoxically, are quite beyond our control. Addiction also makes idolaters of us all, because it forces us to worship these objects of attachment, thereby preventing us from loving God, ourselves, and one another. Addiction breeds willfulness within us, yet, again paradoxically, it erodes our free will and eats away at our dignity. Addiction, then, it at once an inherent part of our nature and an antagonist of our nature. It is the enemy of human freedom and an antagonist of our nature. Yet, in still another paradox, our addictions can lead us to a deep appreciation of grace, the most transformative force in the universe.

Chronically addicted individuals struggle with issues of meaning, identity, and self-worth. Questions such as "Who am I?" and "What is my purpose?" are answered by how individuals handle the challenges of forging a distinct existence across their entire lifespan, from infancy to old age. Navigating the stages of life requires repeated adjustment and accommodation by individuals, particularly as they separate from parents during late adolescence, as they find life partners during early adulthood, determine ways to contribute to society through vocation and parenthood in middle adulthood, and, finally, as they make sense of their life's course in old age.

In life, therefore, people must simultaneously address (1) the limits and possibilities of their particular physical constitution, (2) the limits and possibilities of their own psychological makeup—how they respond to conflict and anxiety and construct meaning out of personal experience—and (3) the limits and possibilities of their particular social contexts—the traditions, expectations, and patterns of their particular family, culture, society, and historical period. The successful navigation of this life journey—determining one's identity—is dependent upon linkage of past, present, and future, upon the contributions of biological, psychological, and social factors at each developmental challenge of life.

If the problem of addiction is attachment—whether adhering to harmful memories and relations, grasping after temporal material things, or clinging to harmful substances and compulsive habits—the solution is detachment, awareness that allegiance to the ego, to physical substances and behavioral patterns that are merely material and temporal, only produce cycles of guilt and despair. Such allegiance might work in the short term, but it cannot ultimately satisfy our lasting nature. The bottom line, then, is conversion, from patterns of behavior and thought that do not satisfy to patterns that work. The transformation, understood psychologically, is from self-centeredness to self-realization; understood metaphorically, from dreaming to awakening; understood socially, from addiction to awareness; understood religiously, from sin to salvation; understood spiritually, from allegiance to ego to allegiance to grace.

When the spiritual traditions of the world speak of detachment, they describe freedom of desire; not freedom *from* desire, but freedom *of* desire. While this idea could be associated with coldness, austerity, and lack of passion, the association is not valid. Detachment aims at preventing one's self from anxious grasping in order to set the spirit free to love and experience love fully. While detachment requires resolve, it involves more than simply letting go of particular patterns and ideas. The truth is that human beings living out of out of ego gratification and self-sufficiency—out of first half of life resources—are powerless to enact the transformation required. Changing from first to second half of life thinking and living requires unlocking the untapped potential and possibilities underlying the temporary, addicted self. Such transformation is not possible unless it is accompanied by awareness of one's true and eternal self.

Entry 2: Awareness and Power

Underlying all addiction are the misuse of power and failure to relinquish control. Wealth, like all material objects, can be addictive; likewise pornography, drugs, gambling, sports, smoking, entertainment, and pleasure. Even religion can be addictive. When temporal entities—and the realms they represent—promise humans abilities and qualities they cannot deliver, such as wealth, happiness, freedom, escape, and fulfillment, they become idols, false gods. This is so because they seek allegiance, promising human mortals qualities they inherently lack—self-fulfillment, self-realization, and self-satisfaction. These false gods are the "powers and principalities" about which believers are warned in the New Testament, termed "cosmic powers of this present darkness" and "spiritual forces of evil" by the author of Ephesians. Ephesians 6:11–17 depicts the warfare of God's people against false powers. Seduced and tempted by the flaming arrows of evil, believers are exhorted to defeat evil by taking on the "whole armor of God," including the belt of truth, the breastplate of righteousness, the shield of faith, and the sword of the Spirit.

The powers of evil are real, as Jesus discovered in the wilderness of Judea and throughout his life, their guarantees formidable—material prosperity, physical prowess, charismatic appeal, political influence (see Luke 4:1–13). While Jesus was offered ultimate authority in exchange for his soul, the powers of evil initially ask of us only minimal allegiance, merely a pound of flesh. For most humans, however, defeat is a matter of time. We succumb because we are inherently weak and incurably turned inward, seeking domination and control over others, circumstances, material objects (which we call "possessions" when they are acquired), and ourselves. We seek control because we have been taught that control brings happiness and success. In actuality, the reverse is true. As spiritual masters indicate, only non-attachment—letting go of control—brings happiness, fulfillment, and peace, because through detachment comes release from fear, stress, insecurity, unhappiness, and lack of fulfillment. When we are weak, the apostle Paul discovered, we are strong.

As psychotherapist Anne Wilson Schaef notes, human society shows all the signs of classic addiction. As we are unable to stop sea levels from rising or prevent other effects of climate change, so we are powerless to stop the waters of our addictive culture from rising. Ignorance, however, is not bliss. If faith can move mountains, one individual can make a difference, and a group of likeminded individuals can change the world. It happened before, and it can happen again.

Essential to the recovery movement known as Alcoholics Anonymous, admitting "powerlessness" and yielding to a Higher Power is the first step to sobriety, for it is only when the recovering alcoholic reaches bottom that transformative power is attained, which includes gaining spiritual meaning that may have been lacking during active alcoholic or drug-using periods. Because addictions represent complex interactions between biological, psychological, social, and spiritual forces, the solution must be holistic as well. The more we understand how addictive enslavement occurs, the better we may be able to turn in the direction of kindness, forgiveness, and service, as the following entries demonstrate.

Entry 3: Awareness and Love

The famous French mathematician and philosopher Blaise Pascal spoke inspirationally when he declared: "There is a God-shaped vacuum in the heart of each person that cannot be satisfied by any created thing but only by God the Creator, made known through Jesus Christ." Psychiatrist Gerald May agrees with Pascal when he writes, "I am convinced that all human beings have an inborn desire for God. Whether we are consciously religious or not, this desire is our deepest longing and our most precious treasure . . . Some of us have repressed this desire, burying it beneath so many other interests that we are completely unaware of it. Or we may experience it in different ways—as a longing for wholeness, completion, or fulfillment. Regardless of how we describe it, it is a longing for love. It is a hunger to love, to be loved, and to move closer to the Source of love. This yearning is the essence of the human spirit, the origin of our highest hopes and most noble dreams."[1]

From a psychoanalytic perspective, we might say that humans displace their longing for God upon other things. Behaviorally, humans are conditioned to seek objects by the positive and negative reinforcements of their own private experience and by the messages of parents, peers, and culture. Even the briefest look at television, magazine, and Internet advertising reveals how strongly culture reinforces attachment to things other than God, and what high value it places on willful self-determination and mastery. Mediating the stimuli they receive, the cells of our brains continually seek equilibrium, developing patterns of adaptation that constitute what is normal. Thus, the more we become accustomed to seeking spiritual satisfaction through things other than God, the more abnormal and stressful it becomes to look for God directly.

When we first reclaim our spiritual longing, we usually do not know that the journey homeward involves relinquishment of self, that the process is so painful and difficult. The greater danger, however, is that those who think they understand the process are likely to try to make it happen on their own, by engaging in false austerities and love-denying deprivations. They will not wait for God's timing; they will rush ahead of grace. This can happen in two ways, when people overinstitutionalize the journey, that is, when people become addicted to religious methods or institutions, or when individuals think they can engineer their own redemption.

1. May, *Addiction and Love*, 1.

However, if we allow grace to guide our response, we will realize what we need to know as we need to know it.

In letting go of addictions, one of the most frightening realizations is that there is no new normality of freedom to replace the old patterns. This lack of normality is actually caused by God, for there can be no addiction to the true God, since God refuses to be an object. While God, perhaps best characterized as "the flow between things," is ever-present, the one passionate and faithful Lover of our lives, God is never ordinary or "normal," and rarely present, as things are present. If lack of normality is true of God, massive implications follow for the conduct of the spiritual life. We all want clear steps to follow, prescribed methods of living and knowing God and staying on track spiritually, but that kind of security and guidance does not exist. Addiction to religious systems, like addiction to anything else, brings slavery, not freedom. The structures of religion are meant to mediate God's self-revelation through community; they are not meant to be substitute gods. Doctrines of belief, moral standards, and reliance on scripture are all essential aspects of authentic spirituality. Sacraments, too, are special means of grace. All are vehicles for God's love, but addiction to them makes them obstacles to the freedom required for growth and transformed lives.

We can temporarily make images of God, freedom, love, and grace, and try to form them into new normalities to which we can cling, but these attachments must eventually be lifted as well. Authentic freedom and love cannot be captured by attachment. Therefore, the journey home does not lead toward new, more sophisticated addictions, or even toward new self-images, for they too can become addictive. While the process of relinquishment—biologically speaking—is really only a matter of easing the power that certain cell systems have over our sense of self—it can feel like death. And it is, spiritually speaking, because without death there can be no resurrection, no lasting transformation. If the journey is truly homeward, it leads toward liberation from addiction altogether. Obviously, this is a lifelong process.

There is a pathetic grandeur in the picture of Adam reaching to taste the fruit of the tree of knowledge of good and evil. Knowledge is humankind's capacity. Freedom to leave the innocence of childhood is precisely what elevates humans above the animals. But when humanity's capacity for knowledge becomes the occasion for arrogant power and self-exaltation, inevitably it results in a fall from the life of trust and goodness that God intends. We cannot recover the mythological innocence of Adam, nor can we return to a Garden that is a figment of the religious imagination. Nevertheless, through revelation humans know there is a better way, the way life can and should be.

While the pattern of the fall ends with the expulsion of Adam and Eve from the Garden, there is good news here. Graciousness appears in the narrative in Genesis 3:21, where God clothes the hapless couple, mercifully shielding them from their shame and giving them a new start, for they get to live and try anew. The ending is hopeful for it represents a new beginning.

Entry 4: Awareness and Need-Love

Whether one views addiction as a disease or as a learning disorder, change (cure) requires five ingredients:

1. Acknowledgment—admitting one has a problem
2. Resolution—willingness to change
3. Substitution—committing to a worthy cause
4. Human help—outside help
5. Divine help—transformative help

Such change—transformation, actually—can only take place if we embark on a spiritual journey, described elsewhere as "the second journey" or "the second half of life." The key to getting unstuck in addiction lies in exchanging our compulsive patterns and behavior for one magnificent obsession, fearlessly staking our claim on the "solution" rather than on the "problem" side of life's ledger. The transformation that brings us to the second half of life is more about unlearning than learning—more about detachment than attachment, about letting go than about grasping or clinging.

This talk of the first and second half of life is not new. It has been embodied for centuries in the scriptures, tales, and experiences of men and women who found themselves on the further journey. In this second half of life, people have less interest in judging or punishing others, or in harboring superiority complexes. The second half of life is not about precepts or commandments, for there is only one guideline: to love the Lord your God with your entire mind, heart, soul, and strength, and your neighbor as yourself.

In his classic study on love, C. S. Lewis notes that God, as creator, implants in humans both "Gift-loves" and "Need-loves."[2] Gift-loves are exhibited naturally, such as in the love of a devoted mother or of a benevolent ruler. In addition to these natural gifts, God bestows "Divine Gift-love," working directly in us. Such love enables us to love lavishly or selflessly, including those who are not naturally loveable (lepers, criminals, enemies). God's Gift-love also enables humans to have Need-love toward God. Thus, God's Gift-love bestows on humans a double Need-love:

- supernatural Need-love of God and

- supernatural Need-love of one another.

Remarkably, God turns our need of God into Need-love of God, and stranger still, creates in us an unnatural receptivity of love from our fellow humans. This includes their love for the unlovable in us. Thus God, admitted to the human heart, transforms not only Gift-love but Need-love; not only our Need-love of God, but our Need-love of one another. And that is the task of true spirituality, the invitation to turn our natural loves into agape love, or more specifically, to let God turn our love into agape. Such a task requires renewal of our hearts and minds, a radical change called conversion, which transforms us from "getting" people to "giving" people. This transformation is beyond human possibility. The Christian message is that humans can only experience this makeover when Christ is "formed" in them (Gal 4:19).

For Lewis, human agape love is not an emotional state but a volitional one, not a state of the feelings but of the will, what we might call "possibility thinking." Agape love is not about liking someone or even about fondness, but rather about "acting as if." In the Bible, one loves God by loving others. And the starting point is to "behave as if" we loved others, because to do so leads to agape. As soon as we engage in such possibility thinking we discover one of life's great truths, that when we behave as if we love someone, we come to love them. The reverse is also true: if we ill-treat others, we come to hate and despise them. And the more cruel we are, the more we will hate—others and God. The key point to remember is that though our feelings for God and others come and go, God's love for us does not.

2. Lewis, *Four Loves*, 176.

Entry 5: Love and Service

In his final message to his friends in recovery, Dr. Bob (cofounder of Alcoholics Anonymous) summarized the Twelve Step program in three phrases—Trust God, Clean House, and Help Others—and in two words—Love and Service. These two concepts, it turns out, summarize Jesus' message regarding human obligation: "you shall love the Lord your God with all your heart, and with all your soul, and with all your strength, and with all your mind; and your neighbor as yourself" (Luke 10:27). Service involves two interrelated dimensions: love of God, manifested in worship, and love of neighbor, manifested in bringing joy to others and in addressing human need. To worship is to experience God, and to experience God is to love and serve others. In the words of Brian McLaren, "There is nothing more radically activist than a truly spiritual life, and there is nothing more truly spiritual than a radically activist life."[3] Victory over addiction, while virtually impossible without outside assistance, becomes practically effortless with divine help.

As people in recovery know, letting go of addiction is not possible without the transformative power of love. By love, I do not mean sentimentality, although human emotion is certainly involved, but unconditional love. The source of such love in the universe, the author of unconditional love, is God. For that reason, when the Bible defines God, it states that God is love (1 John 4:16). Unconditional love (agape), while it cannot be manufactured or produced by mortal creatures, can be displayed by human beings. Such love requires the orientation of one's life toward a center outside of oneself, a recognition that one's value is not absolute but derives from relationship to God. Love can only be acquired in the confidence that it has already been given." As we read in the first epistle of John: "We love, because he first loved us" (1 John 4:19). When we know we are forgiven and loved unconditionally, we come to value other people and things as they are related to God and not as they are useful or important to ourselves. This understanding of love, as divine gift, consistently functions in ways that enable others to flourish with their own dignity and their own relationship to God.

Service is an important tool for remaining free of addictive patterns and behavior. In addition to volunteering locally, such as in food banks, Special Olympics, Cancer Society and American Lung association

---

3. McLaren, *Naked Spirituality*, 237.

programs, helping in nursing homes, visiting the elderly, or participating in other ministries to people in need, there are many options available for doing service through Twelve Step programs in your community. These include becoming a sponsor, volunteering to help with an existing meeting, organizing social events, making phone calls, answering mail, and leading workshops or book studies.

Because of God, the universe is a love-dispensing entity. While ordinary relationships and even sexuality can take place without love, human addiction cannot be defeated without divine love, that is, without God. On their own, out of their own resources, humans may be able to eliminate one or more addictions, but the net result is the substitution of one addiction by another, more virulent type, one form of self-sufficiency and self-control by another. As Einstein noted, "no problem can be solved from the same level of consciousness that created it."

Spirituality and a Holistic Lifestyle

Entry 1: The Good Life

THIS WORLD TEAMS WITH life, thanks to nature and its abundance. The rain falls on every creature, and the sun warms us all. There is a pattern and order to nature that when acknowledged proves to be both generous and hopeful. Humans, following nature, have adopted patterns and rituals that create boundaries and therefore order and meaning to their lives, expressed in families and neighborhoods, societies and nations, and in global citizenship. We have settled into jobs and careers and have devised disciplines, ideologies, religions, arts, technologies, and recreational activities to express our hopes and creative imagination as well as to meet our social, physical, and emotional needs. Life is so good, in fact, that humans have devised ways to enhance and prolong it.

Despite great abundance, nature's goodness seems threatened these days by human waste, negligence, and consumption. If we continue to live arrogantly, selfishly, wastefully, and suspiciously, addicted to violence, chemicals, and hedonistic pursuits, and if we continue to view others as enemies or as inferiors, then the future of humanity and of this planet is bleak. It is not yet too late to change, but if we don't change our attitudes and lifestyles, and do not do so soon, we may reach a hopeless point of no return.

Since the beginning of time, every generation has questioned whether there is a purpose to life, a point to it all. While many people today are skeptical, feeling that life is futile or meaningless, the purpose of religion and philosophy is to posit answers to life's big questions. In *Beyond Belief,* I pondered this issue and concluded that *the purpose of life is to experience Life, for those who experience life fully experience God, who is Life.*[1] I now

---

1. Vande Kappelle, *Beyond Belief,* xviii.

wish to modify that statement, adding moral categories to my definition: *The purpose of life is happiness conducive to the equitable flourishing of all, for God is in all.*[2]

Most human beings desire a good life. Thinking about a good life, how to achieve, maintain, and enhance it, occupies a great deal of our time and attention: we build comfortable homes and secure futures for ourselves; we work hard to advance in our careers; we seek to improve our health and expand our minds; we seek satisfying and enduring relationships with people who value similar goals and activities we enjoy. And because we live in community with others, we think about people whose lives have been shaken by war or violence or natural disasters, and we wonder how their needs relate to our lives.

Although Western ethical concerns have traditionally been voiced in Christian language, we know that this search for inner peace, integrity in relationships, and genuine care for other people is widely shared by our neighbors, whether or not they are Christian. While many people today, religious or secular, think of "the good life" in terms espoused by popular culture, namely as a life built around pleasant and interesting experiences, with enough money and leisure to meet personal desires and familial needs, few thoughtful people try to live a good life on entirely selfish terms. In fact, most of our neighbors of other faiths or of no faith would agree that the good life must include a concern for the well-being of others, peace between nations, and the health of our planet.

According to Eckhart Tolle, the author of the bestselling *The Power of Now*, happiness should be dissociated from life's external conditions, whether positive or negative, and be relegated solely to "inner peace," a nondualist perspective that functions in perfect equanimity beyond pain and suffering

---

2. Though I do not believe in a "personal" God, that is, in a God understandable to human beings and essentially viewed as an "overbig" person, I am not averse to using the term "God." The Bible, both in the Jewish and Christian testaments, declare that "God is Spirit," not person. It was with a metaphysical tradition of personhood in fourth-century Greek theology that calling God "person" took on some meaning. Today, because few of us are metaphysicians of that tradition, we would be better off dropping the notion of the personhood of God and finding a deeper understanding. When we cling to the concept of God as "person," we diminish God's transcendence. Monotheism is to God what a trunk is to a tree. We deceive ourselves if we imagine that the tree is the trunk or that the trunk, being the most visible element of the tree, is therefore the most vital. The tree would be nothing without its roots, which are diverse and rarely visible. In thinking of God, I suggest two metaphors: God is both everywhere to us, like water to fish, but also God is nowhere, like "the void" and "the silence."

and lives "in complete acceptance of what *is*." According to this view, there is no "good" or "bad" in life, there is "only a higher good—which includes the 'bad.'"[3] While I accept the view that there is "a higher good beyond good and bad," I do not limit Tolle's concept of "inner peace" to mental or emotional states only, but understand it in a wider holistic sense as involving external as well as internal factors, as an overall acceptance of well-being that includes peace of body, mind, and spirit.

A good place to start in the journey to happiness is with the question of purpose. What is the purpose of your life? What makes your life meaningful? Whatever your answer, no one chooses to be unhappy, meaning that somehow happiness is central to the issues of personal meaning and purpose. At this point you might wonder, isn't a life based on seeking personal happiness by nature self-centered, even self-indulgent? Not necessarily. As spiritual and psychological studies demonstrate, unhappy people tend to be most self-focused and socially withdrawn. Happy people, by contrast, are generally found to be more sociable, flexible, and creative, able to tolerate life's daily frustrations more easily than unhappy people. More importantly, happy people are found to be more loving and forgiving than unhappy people are.

Entry 2: Holistic Happiness

The Bible as a whole bears witness to the goodness of creation and its fitness for human habitation. If this is a world created as a place for human life, then our search for a good life has to be shaped in the context of a world that is shaped by love. As Robin Lovin indicates in his primer on Christian ethics, "Belief in God as the creator of a good world is less a narrative of how the world came into being than it is a fundamental confidence that we can live our lives in harmony with the natural world around us. . . . The search for a good life is not a struggle to wrest peace and happiness from a hostile or indifferent universe. Belief that God has created us for life in this world suggests also that human good is achieved by . . . a common life in which we may achieve a greater good together than any of us controls alone."[4]

Richard Coan, a professor of psychology at the University of Arizona, spent a large part of his professional career seeking to determine

3. Tolle, *Power of Now*, 178.
4. Lovin, *Christian Ethics*, 13.

the nature of the optimal human personality. He provided a survey of his findings in his 1977 book *Hero, Artist, Sage or Saint?* Coan began by showing that psychology as a science cannot provide the goals for human life. He claimed that if any goals are provided by psychology, the psychologists must either introduce them surreptitiously or openly acknowledge the need for religion and transpersonal meaning.

Coan concluded that there are five elements that characterize the fully developed human person: efficiency, creativity, inner harmony, relatedness, and transcendence. As Coan described these elements, he defined efficiency as the heroic quality. Heroes accomplish things with effectiveness, have strong egos, and are able to focus the direction of their lives. The second element, creativity, is often represented by artists, who are able to present images, poetry, or ideas in a new way so that they touch others with a dimension beyond the physical. The third element is embodied by the sage, the person who has achieved inner harmony. The fourth element, relatedness, is manifested by the saint, the person who treats others with understanding, caring, love, empathy, social sensitivity, and compassion. Saints make other people feel loved and enable them to love. The fifth element is transcendence. This is the vertical aspect of saintliness, whereas relatedness may be considered its horizontal dimension.

Coan suggested that Carl Jung best integrated these concerns in his theory and practice, developing a framework in which all of these have a place. In a 1945 letter Jung wrote to P. W. Martin, a Quaker whose book *Experiment in Depth* was one of the first religious books to acknowledge the religious significance of Jung's work, Jung indicated, "You are quite right. The main interest of my work is not concerned with the treatment of neuroses but rather with the approach to the numinous. But the fact is that the approach to the numinous is the real therapy and inasmuch as you attain to the numinous experiences you are released from the curse of pathology."[5]

For Jung, the human self is the creative principle at the heart of all reality, psychoid (spiritual) and physical. These two aspects of reality can be distinguished, although they interpenetrate one another. Jung usually referred to the spiritual realm as the psychoid. In his letters, he often spoke directly about God, but in most of his published writings he used less religious terminology, hoping to reach the scientific community. According to Jung, human beings are related to and embedded in both the spiritual and physical dimensions of reality. Although he saw the place

5. Jung, *Jung's Letters*, 1:377.

for behavioral, cognitive, existential, and Freudian therapeutic methods for healing patients, he was critical of these methods for claiming to offer exhaustive accounts of the human psyche and for neglecting important data found in the religious understanding of human consciousness. Jung's most important disagreement with non-religious psychological systems was his claim that while human beings are indeed physical creatures, we are also in touch with, surrounded by, and part of a meaningful nonphysical dimension of reality. He believed that unless humans come into touch with God, they are likely to become neurotic. He also believed that the religious and spiritual practice of the Christian church is the best therapeutic system available to human beings. Jung disagreed with those who saw evil only as the absence or deprivation of good. He was convinced that evil is a reality of experience with which humans are required to deal. He also believed that people who venture into the depths of the unconscious confront inner evil, and that they are helpless against it unless they are guided and guarded by a power greater than their own. For this reason, Jung devoted most of the last part of his life to understanding and describing the creative, restoring aspect of the unconscious, utilizing a framework quite similar to that of the New Testament and the teachings and practice of Jesus and of the early church. A remark that Jung made in a British Broadcasting Company Broadcast crystallizes his perspective: "Suddenly I understood that God was, for me at least, one of the most certain and immediate experiences . . . I do not believe; I know. I *know!*"

Entry 3: Holistic Work

Active people do not live in a vacuum. We live in the world, interact with society, have job concerns, money problems, social disagreements, and security issues. In addition, we live with prejudice, racism, sexism, classism, intolerance, poverty, pollution, the disintegration of the family, corporate greed and scandals, unemployment, and widespread job dissatisfaction. Through it all, we need a way to be happy at work as well as at home, and that is not always easy.

Research studies indicate that there is widespread dissatisfaction at work. One recent survey reported that nearly half of American workers are unhappy with their jobs; and things seem to be getting worse. The reasons are varied, ranging from inadequate compensation and boredom to core complex factors related to the specific nature of the work or to workplace conditions. All sorts of things can make someone unhappy at work, including poor social atmosphere, lack of recognition, and monotony. Many workers complain that they lack autonomy, that is, freedom to do their work in their own way. Conversely, others complain that they don't get enough information and direction from their bosses.

Of course, no boss or supervisor can control a worker's attitude. We can all choose to utilize certain inner qualities or spiritual strengths to change our attitude at work or toward bosses and co-workers. Nevertheless, if there is injustice and exploitation, then passive toleration is the wrong response. The appropriate response is to resist it by trying to change the environment rather than accept it. However, if we know there is a higher purpose to our work, and we know that we are doing something useful for society, then that can have a positive effect on our attitude.

In today's workplace environment there is often a focus solely on productivity and on bigger profits. This type of environment leads to much inequity, unfairness, and stress on the employees, and workers must ponder their alternatives. Sometimes we tend to think in black-or-white terms about our jobs, and we must realize that no situation is 100 percent good or 100 percent bad. Everything in life is relative, and it helps to cultivate a wider perspective of the situation. Some jobs may have higher pay, but they come at a price, including longer hours, more responsibility, and possibly risk of injury. When we consider the larger picture, we may discover that while our current work pays less than others, it may come with certain advantages, such as less demands and less danger.

In all cases, contentment is the key. If you have a poor job and the skills and qualifications for better work, then by all means you should exert your best effort for a better job or for a promotion in your current job. However, if you are earning enough to support your family and for your survival, then you need to consider the good aspects of your current situation and realize that you are better off compared to many others. In such situations, a good question to ask is, "Am I permanently happier from the last promotion I received?" Additionally, "Are people situated at higher positions in my place at work happier than those in lower positions?" As recent studies show, people with better paying jobs or more important jobs are no happier in life than those with less important jobs. Surprisingly, findings indicate that while job satisfaction is linked with life satisfaction, the specific type of work one does, including one's occupational prestige, or whether one is blue collar or white collar, has little impact on one's over-all life satisfaction.

Furthermore, if we take a large enough view of things, we notice that all things are interconnected. Often problems in the workplace are caused by factors beyond our control. Perhaps some worldwide economic condition or even certain environmental problems are at the root of the problem. In these cases, it does no good to take things personally. If we feel angry and direct it against others in the workplace, our anger or frustration may only make us more bitter and yet have no effect on the situation or change the wider problems. When workers focus on the larger issue, it creates a sense of unity among them, which creates a sense of greater satisfaction instead of the divisions and conflicts caused when they lose sight of the wider issues and start complaining among themselves. Instead of misplaced anger and frustration, it helps to turn our mental energy in a more constructive direction. This may take some time, but meantime if we can't change the work environment, then we may need to change or adjust our outlook. Otherwise we will remain unhappy at work and in life.

Entry 4: Holistic Aging

In the late 1700s the average life expectancy at birth was 35 years. At the end of the nineteenth century, it was 47 years on average, and only 3 percent of the population made it past age 65. The twentieth-century revolution in longevity led to an added 25 or more years of life. In the United States, average life expectancy at birth has jumped to 76 for males and 81 for females. In addition, people over 85 now constitute the fastest-growing segment of our population. Unfortunately, health maintenance and health promotion among the elderly population have not kept pace. Although it is true that we have postponed death, we have not yet been able to delay the age of onset of a variety of distressing disorders associated with growing older. Dementia, arthritis, diminished hearing and visual acuity, incontinence, and hip fracture all continue to occur at the same ages as in the past.

Does this mean that longer life necessarily brings with it more years of chronic disability? The latest evidence seems to support the concept that it does not and that we can defer disease and dysfunction. Exercise, particularly aerobic activity and resistance training, has been shown to reduce physical frailty, yet 71 percent of people do not exercise. Additionally, disease prevention has increased significantly in the past fifty years; nevertheless, many people do not get vaccines necessary to prevent such diseases as pneumonia and the many strains of the flu. In addition, the vast majority of Americans continue to eat high-fat diets, even though such foods have shown to dramatically increase the risks of heart disease and cancer. It is never too late to introduce new health habits. Indeed, the economic consequences of not doing so and, consequently, of not preventing or postponing dysfunction, are staggering.

Significantly, fifty is considered the new prime of life. At the turn of the twentieth century, one's thirties were looked upon as the key decade during the adult years, that is, the stage when a person was expected to mark his or her major achievements and enjoy the best of health and wisdom. By the middle of the twentieth century, the forties became one's prime decade. Today, thanks to the achievements of modern medicine and an unparalleled standard of living, we can expect our second fifty years to be as rich and full as the first. Of course, this does not mean that age does not bring changes, or that we can breeze through our mature years painlessly. Nor does it change the fact that we live in a youth-oriented society. But today people in their sixties and even older run marathons, earn college degrees, start new businesses, travel around the world, and experience the enthusiasm and excitement of new ventures.

Nutrition is an important aspect of health, and how we eat, whether too much, not enough, or just right, is often an effective indicator of a healthy lifestyle. A basic principle in eating holistically is to consider eating from a sacramental point of view. Viewing eating from a sacramental point of view grants us freedom but also responsibility.

Each of us has a unique physique, metabolism, and appetite. Encompassing these qualities is the Aristotelian proviso of moderation or "the mean." In terms of eating, what this means is that what is sufficient or appropriate for one person may not be adequate for another, and what one person considers wholesome, nutritious, and edible may not suit another. Only you can decide how to eat sacramentally. To do so mindfully, remember that quantities and foods that were once adequate and healthy may not be so today or tomorrow. In addition, eat lots of fruit, vegetables, and whole grains, in addition to a variety of protein such as seafood, lean meats, poultry, eggs, legumes, soy products, low-fat yogurt, and nuts and seeds. To stay within your daily calory needs, avoid overeating. If your favorite recipes call for fried fish or breaded chicken, try healthier variations by baking or grilling.

To obtain the nutrients and other substances needed for good health, vary the foods that you eat. Healthy eating is about balance. You can enjoy your favorite comfort foods, even if they are high in calories, fat, or added sugars. The key is eating them less often and in smaller quantities, and balancing them with healthier foods and increased physical activity. Remember to avoid highly processed foods, added sugars, baked sweets, salty snacks, sweetened drinks, and alcoholic beverages.

Many Americans gain weight in adulthood, increasing their risk for high blood pressure, heart disease, stroke, diabetes, certain types of cancer, arthritis, breathing problems, and other illnesses. Therefore, most adults should not gain weight. If you are overweight and have one of these problems, you should try to lose weight, or at the very least, not gain weight.

In all cases, learn to listen to your body to notice whether you are truly hungry or not, and if you are, be mindful of what foods you choose to eat. Be aware when it's time to stop eating, as well as when you eat for reasons other than hunger. If you are eating for emotional reasons, consider bringing self-inquiry to the emotions, rather than soothing them or dulling yourself with food. If you are eating or drinking for a quick energy boost or to change your mental state or mood, focus on your situation and understand the feelings that may fuel unhealthy habits. If you need energy, perhaps more rest or a regimen of healthy exercise is the answer.

The previously held view that increased risk of diseases and disability with advancing age results from inevitable, intrinsic aging processes, for the most part genetically determined, is inconsistent with a developing body of information that many aging characteristics are due to lifestyle and are not age-dependent. Included among these are maintenance of interpersonal relations and of productive activities such as developing hobbies and unpaid volunteer work.

Reduced muscle strength in older people is a major cause of the increased prevalence of the functional disability found in this population. Muscle strength forms a critical component of mobility, and the high prevalence of falls among institutionalized elders may be a consequence of reduced muscle strength. Over the past several decades, evidence has been accumulating to indicate that a positive correlation exists between physical activity and the reduction in risk of such chronic diseases as coronary heart disease, hypertension, and osteoporosis.

Aerobic exercise is an important means of preventing and treating many of the chronic diseases typically associated with old age. If physical activity reduces the risk of developing these chronic diseases, it is logical to assume that premature mortality—from any cause—can be averted or at least delayed by physical activity. Consequently, physical activity can be expected to enhance longevity. While exercise cannot guarantee longevity to all, middle-aged individuals might expect to gain, on average, some two years of life from being physically active. It is encouraging to note that even older individuals benefit from a physically active life and that the process of healthy aging can begin at any age.

Almost any physical activity will suffice, and there is no need to push yourself until you are gasping for air. You don't even need to return from your session soaked in sweat. Yes, you do get extra benefit from exercising harder or longer, but that benefit is small compared to the benefit you apparently get from moderate exercise. You can still get real cardiovascular benefit from an easy thirty-minute bike ride; however, the key with mild levels of activity is that they need to occur frequently. Instead of a long walk, you can take three ten-minute walks a day, or ride a bike for twenty minutes and walk for ten.

Entry 5: Holistic Creativity

Creativity is an experience—a spiritual experience. At first, each of us receives a task: to be our unique selves by creating a life never before lived. As the painter Pablo Picasso quipped, "Every child is an artist. The problem is how to remain an artist when he (or she) grows up."

According to seminal teacher and artist Julia Cameron, creative artists dwell in the presence of something transcendent—in the realm of spiritual electricity—and the heart of creativity is an experience of mystical union with a transcendent entity some call God but also Great Creator, Higher Power, Divine Spirit, Source, Mind, Universe, Deity, and Goddess. Like electricity, we don't need to understand Deity to utilize its power and grace. Those who speak in spiritual terms routinely refer to God as Creator and to themselves as co-creators or sub-creators, forging a creative alliance, artist-to-artist with the Great Creator. According to Cameron, accepting the following basic principles of creativity can greatly expand our creative possibilities:[6]

1. Creativity is the natural order of life, for life is pure creative energy.

2. There is an underlying, in-dwelling creative force infusing all life—including ourselves.

6. The following principles are adapted from Cameron, *Artist's Way*, 3.

3. When we open to our creativity, we open to the Creator's creativity within us.

4. As creations of God, we are meant to continue creativity by being creative.

5. Creativity is God's gift to us; using our creativity is our gift back to God.

6. Refusing to be creative is selfish and counter to our true nature.

7. When we explore our creativity, we open to God's orderly direction.

8. As we open our creative channel to the Creator, we can expect gentle yet powerful changes to our nature.

9. We are safe when we yield to ever-greater creativity.

10. Our creative dreams and yearnings come from a divine source; as we open to our dreams, we open toward our divinity.

One of the chief barriers to accepting God's generosity is our limited notion of what we are able to accomplish. We may tune in to the voice of the Creator within, hear a message, and then discount it as impossible. It is understandable that we might not want to look like idiots pursuing grandiose schemes. However, if we don't take ourselves—or God—seriously enough, we might define as impossible opportunities that, with God's help, may fall withing our grasp. Remembering that God is our source, we are in the spiritual position of having an unlimited bank account. Most of us never consider how powerful the Creator is, and thereby draw very limited amounts of the power available to us. When we decide how powerful God is for us, we unconsciously set limits on how much God can give us or help us. And if we receive gifts beyond our imagining, we often send them back.

Creativity is a spiritual issue. Any progress we make is by leaps of faith, some small and some large. And that faith begins with taking the first step toward learning a new medium. Later, that faith may lead to classes, seminars, and possibly a year's sabbatical. Still later we may conceive an idea for a book, or artistic space in an art gallery exhibit. If this sounds unreachable, ask yourself bluntly what steps you are evading and what dreams you are discounting. With God as our source, all things are possible.

In the Sermon on the Mount, Jesus encourages his followers to seek first God's kingdom (God's will), and all other things will be given to them as well (Matt 6:33). Sometimes we limit "all other things" to the realm of spirituality, but to do so is to go against the context of the passage. God is not a stern parent with rigid ideas about what's socially acceptable or politically correct. God wants us to live life fully, and that certainly implies areas such as creative writing, art, and dance. Living artistically means getting into the now and enjoying our day. It begins with giving ourselves treats and breaks. God is a God of extravagance and abundance, and we should learn to be extravagant with ourselves and with others. As we expect God to be more generous, God will be more generous to us.

Once we accept that it is natural to create, we can begin to accept a second idea—that the Creator will hand us whatever we need for the project. The minute we are willing to accept the help of this collaborator, we begin to see useful bits of help everywhere in our lives. If we remember that God is the Great Artist, then we can expect the universe to support our dream.

Creativity is oxygen for the soul. Cutting off creativity makes people unhappy, depressed, or angry. When well-meaning parents and friends push marriage or nine-to-five jobs on them, artists react as if they are fighting for their lives, for they are. To be an artist is to question accepted standards, to recognize the particular, to appreciate the peculiar. To be an artist is to acknowledge the astonishing. It is to allow the wrong piece in a room if we like it, or to cling to a weird coat, hat, or other piece of clothing that makes us happy. If we are happier writing than not writing, painting than not painting, singing than not singing, dancing than not dancing, acting than not acting, the by all means we must allow ourselves to do it. To kill our dreams because they are irresponsible is to be irresponsible to ourselves. Credibility lies with us and God—not with votes of approval from others.

The Creator made us creative. Our creativity is our gift from God. Our use of it is our gift to God. The artist's way is a spiritual journey, a pilgrimage home to the self. As creators bearing the divine image, human beings are co-creators with God. That's why we were created. When we experience creativity, the disruption might make us feel we are losing our mind—or gaining our soul. While many of us are cautious about taking risks or being creative in personal or spiritual aspects of our lives, such ways of living and thinking are inevitable for second half of life spirituality. As we move into second half of life living and thinking, we no longer need permission to be creative. Such permission and encouragement, we discover have been latent in our spiritual DNA all along.

Bibliography

Allison Jr., Dale C. *The Luminous Dusk: Finding God in the Deep, Still Places.* Grand Rapids, MI: Eerdmans, 2006.

Bass, Diana Butler. *Christianity After Religion: The End of Church and the Birth of a New Spiritual Awakening.* New York: HarperOne, 2012.

Borg, Marcus, and N. T. Wright. *The Meaning of Jesus: Two Visions.* San Francisco: HarperSanFrancisco, 2000.

Bourgeault, Cynthia. *The Heart of Centering Prayer: Nondual Christianity in Theory and Practice.* Boulder, CO: Shambhala, 2016.

———. *The Holy Trinity and the Law of Three.* Boston, Shambhala, 2013.

Cameron, Julia. *The Artist's Way: A Spiritual Path to Higher Creativity.* 10th anniversary ed. New York: Tarcher/Putnam, 2002.

Campbell, Joseph. *The Hero's Journey: Joseph Campbell on His Life and Work.* Edited by Phil Cousineau. Novato, CA: New World Library, 2003.

———. *The Inner Reaches of Outer Space: Metaphor as Myth and as Religion.* Novato, CA: New World Library, 2002.

———. *The Power of Myth: with Bill Moyers.* New York: Doubleday, 1988.

———. *Romance of the Grail: The Magic and Mystery of Arthurian Myth.* Novato, CA: New World Library, 2015.

———. *Thou Art That: Transforming Religious Metaphor.* Novato, CA: New World Library, 2001.

Dalai Lama, and Howard C. Cutler. *The Art of Happiness: A Handbook for Living.* New York: Riverhead, 1009.

———. *The Art of Happiness at Work.* New York: Riverhead, 2003.

Dunn, Stephen, and Anne Lonergan. *Befriending the Earth.* Mystic, CT: Twenty-Third Publications, 1991.

Dychtwald, Ken. *Healthy Aging: Challenges and Solutions.* Gaithersburg, MD: Aspen, 1999.

Esposito, John, et al. *World Religions Today.* New York: Oxford University Press, 2001.

Fowler, James. *Stages of Faith: The Psychology of Human Development and the Quest for Meaning.* San Francisco: HarperSanFrancisco, 1995.

Fox, Matthew. *Creation Spirituality.* New York: HarperSanFrancisco, 1991.

———. *Original Blessing.* Santa Fe, NM: Bear & Co., 1983.

Haught, John. *The Promise of Nature: Ecology and Cosmic Purpose.* Mahwah, NJ: Paulist, 1993.

Hollis, James. *Finding Meaning in the Second Half of Life: How to Finally, Really Grow Up.* New York: Gotham, 2006.

———. *The Middle Passage: From Misery to Meaning in Midlife.* Toronto: Inner City Books, 1993.

Homes, Urban T. *The History of Christian Spirituality.* New York: Seabury, 1980.

Jung, Carl G. *AION: Researches into the Phenomenology of the Self.* In *Collected Works*, 9:2. New York: Pantheon, 1953.

———. *Jung's Letters.* Vol 1. Edited by Gerhard Adler and Aniela Jaffé. Princeton, NJ: Princeton University Press, 1975.

———. *Memories, Dreams, Reflections.* New York: Pantheon, 1963.

———. *Modern Man in Search of a Soul.* New York: Harcourt, Brace and World, Inc., 1933.

Kasser, Tim. *The High Price of Materialism.* Cambridge, MA: The MIT Press, 2002.

Kelsey, Morton T. *Companions on the Inner Way: The Art of Spiritual Guidance.* New York: Crossroad, 1983.

Lesser, Elizabeth. *The Seeker's Guide: Making Your Life a Spiritual Adventure.* New York: Villard, 2000.

Lewis, C. S. *The Abolition of Man.* New York: Macmillan, 1947.

———. *The Four Loves.* New York: Harcourt Brace, 1960.

Lindesmith, A. R. *Addiction and Opiates.* Chicago: Aldine, 1968.

Lovin, Robin W., *Christian Ethics: An Essential Guide.* Nashville, TN: Abingdon, 2000.

May, Gerald G. *Addiction and Grace.* New York: HarperOne, 1991.

McLaren, Brian D. *Faith After Doubt: Why Your Beliefs Stopped Working and What to Do About It.* New York: St. Martin's, 2021.

———. *Naked Spirituality.* San Francisco: HarperOne, 2011.

Newell, John Philip. *The Rebirthing of God: Christianity's Struggle for New Beginnings.* Woodstock, VT: Skylight Paths, 2014.

Palmer, Helen. *The Enneagram: Understanding Yourself and the Others in Your Life.* San Francisco: HarperSanFrancisco, 1991.

Peck, M. Scott. *The Different Drum.* New York: Simon & Schuster, 1987.

Peele, Stanton, and Archie Brodsky. *Love and Addiction.* New York: New American Library, 1976.

Plotkin, Bill. *Nature and the Human Soul: Cultivating Wholeness and Community in a Fragmented World.* Novato, CA: New World Library, 2008.

———. *Soulcraft: Crossing into Mysteries of Nature and Psyche.* Novato, CA: New World Library, 2003.

Riso, Don Richard, and Russ Hudson. *Personality Types: Using the Enneagram for Self-Discovery.* Rev. ed. New York: Houghton Mifflin, 1996.

———. *Understanding the Enneagram.* Rev. ed. New York: Houghton Mifflin, 2000.

———. *The Wisdom of the Enneagram.* New York: Bantam, 1999.

Rohr, Richard. *Eager to Love: The Alternative Way of Francis of Assisi.* Cincinnati, OH: Franciscan Media, 2014.

———. *The Enneagram: A Christian Perspective.* Rev. ed. New York: Crossroad, 2001.

———. *Falling Upward: A Spirituality for the Two Halves of Life.* San Francisco: Jossey-Bass, 2011.

———. *Immortal Diamond: The Search for Our True Self.* San Francisco: Jossey-Bass, 2013.

———. *The Naked Now: Learning to See as the Mystics See.* New York: Crossroad, 2009.

———. *Quest for the Grail*. New York: Crossroad, 1994.

———. *The Universal Christ*. New York: Convergent, 2019.

———. *What the Mystics Know*. New York: Crossroad, 2015.

Smith, Huston. *Forgotten Truth: The Common Vision of the World's Religions*. San Francisco: HarperSanFrancisco, 1976.

———. *Why Religion Matters*. San Francisco: HarperSanFrancisco, 2001.

———. *The World's Religions*. San Francisco: HarperSanFrancisco, 1991.

Szalavitz, Maia. *Unbroken Brain: A Revolutionary New Way of Understanding Addiction*. New York: St. Martin's, 2016.

Tolle, Eckhart. *The Power of Now: A Guide to Spiritual Enlightenment*. Novato, CA: New World Library, 1999.

Vande Kappelle, Robert P. *Addiction: How We Get Stuck and Unstuck in Compulsive Patterns and Behavior*. Eugene, OR: Wipf & Stock, 2019.

———. *Adventures in Spirituality: A Journey from Belief to Faith*. Eugene, OR: Wipf & Stock, 2020.

———. *Beyond Belief: Faith, Science, and the Value of Unknowing*. Eugene, OR: Wipf & Stock, 2012.

———. *Dark Splendor: Spiritual Fitness for the Second Half of Life*. Eugene, OR: Resource, 2015.

———. *Heart to Heart: The Journey Outward*. Eugene, OR: Wipf & Stock, 2023.

———. *Holistic Happiness: Spirituality and a Healing Lifestyle*. Eugene, OR: Wipf & Stock, 2022.

———. *In the Potter's Workshop*. Eugene, OR: Wipf & Stock, 2019.

———. *Living Graciously on Planet Earth: Faith, Hope, and Love in Biblical, Social, and Cosmic Context*. Eugene, OR: Wipf & Stock, 2016.

———. *Into Thin Places: One Man's Search for the Center*. Eugene, OR: Resource, 2010.

———. *Wading in Water: Spirituality in the Arts*. Eugene, OR: Wipf & Stock, 2021.

———. *Walking on Water: Living into a New Way of Thinking*. Eugene, OR: Wipf & Stock, 2020.

Weiss, Robert J., and Genell J. Subak-Sharpe. *Complete Guide to Health and Well-Being After 50*. New York: Times, 1988.

Wiman, Christian. *My Bright Abyss: Meditation of a Modern Believer*. New York: Farrar, Strauss and Giroux, 2013.

Index

Abraham, 43
Adam and Eve, 4, 125
addiction, 107–21
    and consumerism, 116–18
    overcoming, 119–28
aging, holistic, 135–38
agnosticism, 21, 23
Alcoholics Anonymous, 122, 127
Allison Jr., Dale, 88, 89
alternative orthodoxy, 74
apophatic, 104
Aristotle, 91
Athanasius, 56
Augustine of Hippo, 5, 83

Bass, Diana Butler, 10
belief(s), ix, x, 13–15, 38, 79
Berry, Thomas, 4, 86
binary perspective. *See* dualism, dualistic
Blake, William, 61
Bonhoeffer, Dietrich, x
Bourgeault, Cynthia, 65, 75
Buddha, the, 3, 20, 58, 62
Buddhism, 3, 69

Cameron, Julia, 138
Chopra, Deepak, 39
Christendom, 95
Christianity, viii, 14–15, 84, 95
    and Judaism, 14
    religionless, x
    stages of development, 2
church, x, 24
circle of fifths, 54

Coan, Richard, 131–32
competing points of view, 74
    See also four points of view
consumerism, 116–18
conversion, religious, 22, 52, 62, 79, 82, 95, 126
creativity, 132, 138–40

Daoism (Taoism), 3, 69
    See also Tao
Dobzhansky, Theodosius, 74
dualism, dualistic, ix, 15, 16, 45, 47, 48, 49, 50, 61, 64–68, 78, 83, 92, 93, 109
    overcoming, 68–72

ego, 3, 7, 31, 32, 39, 47, 51, 53, 55, 57, 58, 60, 80, 83, 120, 121
Einstein, Albert, 74, 128
Eliade, Mircea, 15
Eliot, T. S., 92
Enlightenment, 2
Enneagram, the, 105–6
Erikson, Erik, 20, 32, 36
Esposito, John 16, 17
ethics, ethical, 43–44
evil, 121, 122, 133
exercise, 137–38
existential (ultimate) questions, 73, 82

faith, ix, 38, 49, 51, 79, 83, 139
    critical, 21, 22, 50
    journey of, vii, viii, xi, 7, 19–23, 38, 43, 47–53, 64, 79

faith *(continued)*
    postcritical, 21, 23
    precritical, 21
false self, 3, 7, 31, 39, 53, 55–60
    death of, 57–59
fifth dimension, 54
first half of life, x, 3, 8, 24, 25, 27, 28, 29,
        39, 44, 48, 49, 52, 58, 73, 95, 103,
        121, 125
four points of view, 74–76
Fowler, James, xi, 36–37, 44, 45, 48, 51
Fox, Matthew, 4, 7
Freud, Sigmund, 23, 99, 133
fundamentalism, 2, 9, 64, 84

global health, 72
God, xi, 3, 18, 21, 50, 75, 76, 79, 80, 104,
        108, 123, 124, 132, 133, 139
    awareness of, consciousness of, 39, 43
    as Creator, 79, 87, 91, 123, 131, 138,
        139, 140
    and evil, 121–22
    human dependence on, 5
    image of, 3, 7, 62, 66, 140
    as immanent and transcendent, 85
    knowing, 7, 22, 51, 124
    as Life, 129
    love for, 5, 7, 8, 22
    love of, vii, 5, 22, 124, 126, 127
    and Need-love, 126
    oneness of, 74
    as personal, 76, 130n2
good life, the, 129–31
Grail quest, 92–95
Gurdjieff, George, 105

happiness, 117, 122, 130, 131–33
Haught, John F., 75, 87, 88
heaven, 60, 62, 65, 69, 70
Hegel, G. W. F., 20, 75
hell, 60
Hindu, Hinduism, 41–42, 44, 45, 47, 48,
    51, 63, 66, 69, 70, 74, 83, 84
Hollis, James, 31
Holmes, Urban, 75, 104–5
Holy Spirit, 6, 7, 38, 39, 48, 52, 58, 76,
    77, 78

Hugh of St. Victor, 61
human development, models of, 32–35
human identity, 3–4
Huvelin, Abbé, 23

Irenaeus, 56

Jesus Christ, ix, 20, 55, 58, 70–72, 75, 91,
    96, 123
    belief in, ix, 14
    death and resurrection of, 58, 60
    as healer, 39
    as Logos, 70
    as Messiah, 14
    as Redeemer, 14
    and religious heritage, 56, 57
    and spirituality, 60, 61
JHWH, 74
John of the Cross, 66
Jonah, sign of, 58
Judaism, 12, 13–14
Julian of Norwich, 66
Jung, Carl, 23, 31, 75, 99, 100, 102, 103,
    104, 132–33

Kasser, Tim, 117, 118
kataphatic, 104
Kelsey, Morton, 23
Kierkegaard, Søren, 42–44, 45, 47, 49, 51
kingdom of God, x, 62, 72, 96, 139
koan, 53
Kohlberg, Lawrence, 33, 36, 44, 45, 47,
    48, 51

Lao Tzu, 82
Lectio Divina, 74
Lesser, Elizabeth, 77
levels of reality, 76–78
Lewis, C. S., 70, 97, 126
Lindesmith, Alfred, 109
love, vii, 7, 51, 60, 123–28, 132
    and addiction, 115–16
    agape (divine), vii, x, 126, 127
Lovin, Robin, 131
Loyola, Ignatius, 6

Maimonides, Moses, 5

Marx, Karl, 20
May, Gerald, 123
MBTI (Myers Briggs Type Indicator), 75,
    100–3, 104
McLaren, Brian, 75, 127
Meister Eckhart, 66
Merton, Thomas, 55
models (stages) of
    faith, 19–20, 36–37, 47–53
    human development, 31–35
    life, 24–30, 41–42
    spirituality, 20–30, 42–44, 44–53
monism, 66, 69, 70
myth, mythology, 59, 90–91

Nasr, Seyyed, 81
Neumann, John von, 67
Newell, John Philip, 4
Newton, Isaac, 86
Nietzsche, Friedrich, 38
nondual. *See* unitive consciousness
nutrition, 136–37

Otto, Rudolph, 59

Palmer, Helen, 106
panentheism, x, 5
paths to meaning, 73–74
Paul (apostle), 14, 22, 51, 56, 62, 65, 96,
    122
Peck, M. Scott., 37
Peele, Stanton, 115
Perennial Tradition, 79, 81–84
person(hood), 3–4
Picasso, Pablo, 138
Plotkin, Bill, 25, 34–35
polarities. *See* dualism, dualistic
polytheism, 12
postmodern, 2, 20
prayer, 29
primal, x, 1, 92

Rahner, Karl, 57
religio, 9, 10
religion, ix, 2, 57, 62, 68, 82, 84, 132
    ancient pagan, 13–15
    healthy and "junk," 17–18

inadequate, 58, 64
mature, 57, 58
as noun or adjective, 15–17
primal, x, 1, 11–12
role of, 9–11
sacramental role of, 87–88
Richard of St. Victor, 61
Richardson, Peter Tufts, 75
Ricoeur, Paul, 27
Rowling, J. K., 97

salvation, 15, 60, 121
Schaef, Anne Wilson, 122
second half of life, viii, x, 3, 8, 19, 24–30,
    38, 39, 44, 48, 50, 52, 95, 102, 103,
    121, 125, 140
self(hood), 76–78
Sermon on the Mount, 139
shadow self, 58n4
sin, 43, 77, 80, 108, 121
Singh, Kathleen Dowd, 60
Smith, Huston, 76–78
Smith, Wilfred Cantwell, 9–10, 69
Socrates, 43
soul, 25, 52, 76, 78, 140
spiritual, xi, 5, 10, 140
    growth, viii, xi, 8, 19
    transformation, vii, viii, 55, 56, 58,
      59, 62, 70–72, 82, 83, 87, 121, 125
spirituality, viii, xi, 1, 2, 5, 6, 8, 9, 10,
    48–49, 51, 54, 68, 78, 84, 90, 95,
    98, 124, 139, 140
    definition of, 5–7, 39, 58
    goal of, 8
    and a holistic lifestyle, 129–40
    and personality, 99–106
    role of, 55, 58
    stages of, 39–40
    task of, 8, 126
    See also models of
Szalavitz, Maia, 110

Tao, the, 69, 70, 83
Teresa of Ávila, 66
ternary perspective, 75–76
theology, x
theosis, 56

thin places, 95–98
Tolle, Eckhart, 130, 131
Trinity, 75
True Self, 7, 53, 55–60, 63, 93
    resurrection of, 59–60
truth, religious, viii, 63, 79, 84, 91

unitive consciousness, viii, ix, x, 50, 51,
    65–67, 69–70, 83, 92

Wilber, Ken, 27
Wiman, Christian, viii
work, holistic, 133–35

yin and yang, 69